COOKING from SCRATCH

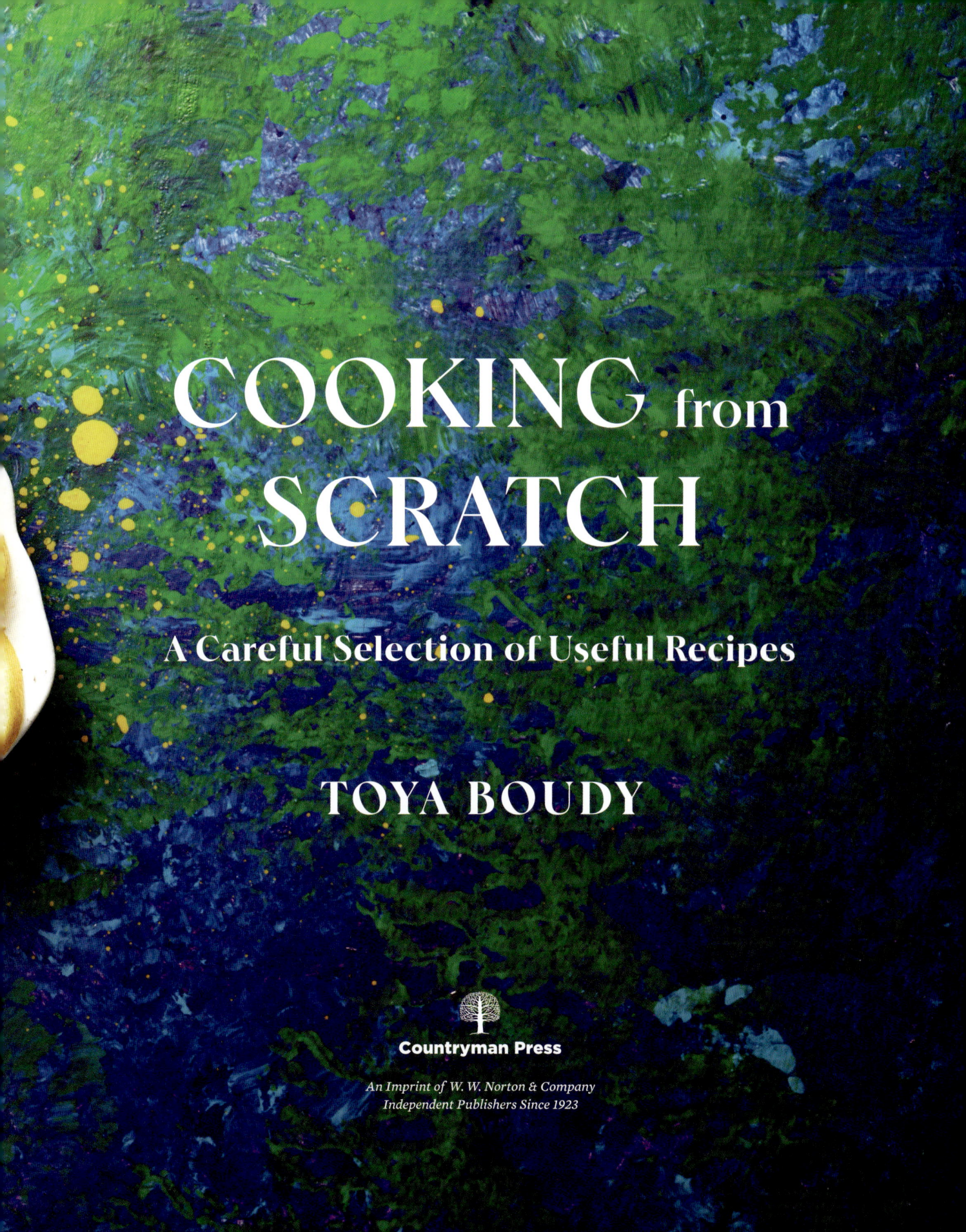

COOKING from SCRATCH

A Careful Selection of Useful Recipes

TOYA BOUDY

Countryman Press

An Imprint of W. W. Norton & Company
Independent Publishers Since 1923

For information about permission to reproduce selections from this book, write to Permissions, Countryman Press, 500 Fifth Avenue, New York, NY 10110

For information about special discounts for bulk purchases, please contact W. W. Norton Special Sales at specialsales@wwnorton.com or 800-233-4830

Manufacturing by Toppan Leefung Pte. Ltd.
Book design by Allison Chi
Production manager: Devon Zahn

Countryman Press
www.countrymanpress.com

An imprint of W. W. Norton & Company, Inc.
500 Fifth Avenue, New York, NY 10110
www.wwnorton.com

Authorized EU representative: EAS, Mustamäe tee 50, 10621 Tallinn, Estonia

978-1-324-11161-0

1 2 3 4 5 6 7 8 9 0

To myself: Toya, you did it; it felt like you couldn't but you did. I want you to always remember that you are that rose that grew from concrete. If there isn't any light to be seen, you will always choose to be it. Thank you for never giving up on the vision.

To the readers: I wrote this book to be a village or a shoulder for you to lean on. A written elder to impart wisdom and knowledge on you at the perfect time. I pray that this book comes in handy when you need a helping hand.

WISDOM FROM MY MAMA

If anything happens where you don't have the money, you can cook from scratch. If you need to heal your body, you can watch everything going into your body by cooking from scratch. If you're starting over in a new place, you better get the main ingredients in your cabinets so you can cook something from scratch if all else fails. You see, it's nice to have money to do it quickly, but sometimes you need to just cook from scratch. It's just better that way.

—Emily Delahoussaye Thomas

CONTENTS

INTRODUCTION

I wrote this book from a place of starting over. During the past year, I went through a divorce, my mama fought for her life through multiple brain surgeries after a brain bleed and a stroke, we sold our home, moved into new ones, and had to figure out new family routines. Month after month, my days were filled with daily roller coasters, sitting sandwiched between the questions "What if I'm wrong? And what if I'm right?" Then, I splashed into a pool filled with the daunting question that we all fear: "What's next?"

Did I make it out okay? I did. I'm well, whole, and ready to share, simply because there's no way I'd walk through so much fire without coming back without a map and tips to help you not get as burned as I did, and to help you rebuild faster.

I found myself starting over in a way I haven't done since my twenties. In my case, I faced moving boxes, empty cabinets, furniture that needed to be assembled, and forgetting to buy the simple needs like soap, salt, and paper towels, because I was managing a series of spinning plates while standing barefoot hoping I wouldn't sneeze. I'm thankful to say that we all made it through.

I know I'm not the only person who ever started over. There are many different sorts of starting over as well—it could be as simple as stocking the fridge for the first time in a new home or having the urge to purge and try something different. For me, it was dramatic, but I hope the recipes in this book can help anyone at any point in their lives to keep moving forward with grace and self-empathy.

While I was going through these challenges, I came across a book by Malinda Russell. Long out of print, this guide to cooking, home remedies, and perseverance struck me as a great model for my book. Malinda was the first free woman of color to publish a cookbook, called *A Domestic Cook Book: Containing a Careful Selection of Useful Receipts for the Kitchen* in 1866. I caught that it was a guide, a helpmate, or you could even call it a village in the form of a cookbook for the readers. It was written in the language of that time, with the solutions many of her people needed. It was groundbreaking, to me, for her to write a book with so much knowledge, covering all areas of life. Malinda learned to cook while working for a wealthy Virginia family, then married and had a child. Her husband died, and her son was disabled, but she continued to live her life, looking to her dream of moving to Liberia. She operated a boardinghouse and pastry shop in Tennessee, where she wrote her book. In her travels as a single mother, she was robbed and her life was threatened, but she continued on. Malinda never made it to Liberia, but adapted and accepted the life she had as an author and member of her community. Her voice was strong and certain on the page, and it inspired me to keep going and hold tight to belief.

Both Malinda and I had to embrace starting over and weathering the storms of new beginnings. What do we need during these times? Help, wisdom, and guidance. Sometimes, it bubbles up from within; other times, we learn from the mouths and hands of others willing to gift us life lessons. It was her knowledge about food, remedies, and principles that gave Malinda the greatest support. That's what I want to pass on to you.

This book will help you with a fresh start, no matter where you are in your journey of life. My chapters are inspired by Malinda's wide net—she included everything from a basic cake recipe to healing tonics to special hair treatments—but the focus is on the kitchen and cooking. As my parents always said, "You gotta eat!"

In this book, I will share the best ways to stock a kitchen, recipes to learn by heart, recipes that speak to my sense of home, and recipes to share with friends and family. I'll also include some basic home remedies and throw in a few recipes for homemade cleaning solutions, bath salts, and shampoos. I like the idea of helping people discover their own peace, starting with a clean kitchen, a solid meal, and a healthy tonic before bed.

Home

Whenever we start over, we are essentially looking for a new place to call home within a situation or circumstance. A safe spot that births a new normalcy. "Home" was a floating label for me in my twenties. I was evicted from every place that I rented because it took over 20 jobs and pink slips to realize I was an artist and that I would have a hard time molding to the normal way of doing things, on top of being displaced by a hurricane for a few years. I don't think I thought about the word "home" in a sense of it being my permanent spot; I'd say I thought of it as wherever I rested at the time.

In the midst of moving around and starting over frequently, I adapted to the changes by becoming "home." I became home by rapidly accepting the circumstances and making peace with change and time. That's a mouthful, I know, but to make peace with change and time is to not fight the flow and war with what was or could have been in your eyes. It's letting go of what you hoped for and being grate-

ful for what is right in front of you and making the most out of every moment.

For me, that looked like simple celebrations. I became a parent at 16 years old; it was just us two for a long time, and I knew that our "normal" looked really different from the other families my daughter Heaven saw at school, so I'd try to make things our own kind of special. For example, I would celebrate by making something my daughter wanted for dinner or as a movie snack. There was a gas station I worked at and after my shift, I would get cool snacks and neatly pack them in a brown paper bag for her. It was incredibly simple, but after school, it felt like a prize bag of goodies waiting for her. We also loved going for a ride and eating in the car; it was so comforting. You know, I never thought about how we started doing that in the first place; it was after being displaced after Hurricane Katrina. This was one of our big start-over points, when all our belongings were packed tightly into a 1988 Camry we called "The Blue Beast." That car became a safe space, a dining room in a sense, because we slept on someone's couch together and we weren't the only evacuees, so the living quarters were pretty snug with people. Essentially, that front seat was what felt like "home" to us until I got us an apartment.

You see, there are many ways you can find home away from the conventional idea of home. That's what we are all looking for when we are starting from scratch—we're looking to create that space called home. I believe that whether we are starting over by way of it being the first time doing something, heartbreak, trauma, or rebuilding in place, we all deserve that calm sunshine after the storm of change.

Now, years later, I've also witnessed my older daughter, Heaven, get her apartment for the first time! I walked in and saw the empty cabinets and remembered the work it took to figure out what to

buy and when. I even recalled how expensive it is to buy all the odds and ends you don't remember until you cut your finger or need to open a can last minute.

I had a conversation with my daughter at some point and mentioned to her we all are learning this stuff for the first time! We aren't born knowing how to stock a cabinet or make a roux. It's not so much that the information is hidden from us; we simply don't think to ask for help in that specific way. And, most times, the people around us are just waiting for the invitation to give advice, trying not to overstep.

With that being said, I think it's a perfect fit for me to include a simple "how to stock a kitchen" guide. Use it as a template, take out what you don't need, and add whatever you want. I just want to give you a general idea of what getting started will look like.

Stock the Kitchen

You just moved into a new place, or have decided you want to get organized. To me, the best way to feel settled in your home and in your heart is by stocking the kitchen!

Fridge Day-One Musts

Even before a full grocery stock-up, grab:

Bottled or filtered water jug

Milk or milk alternative

Eggs

Butter or margarine

Bread

A few frozen meals (for move-in days)

Kitchen Cabinet (Dry Pantry Basics)

Think: shelf-stable foods that last and build meals

Grains & Starches

Rice (white or brown)

Pasta (spaghetti and one short shape)

All-purpose flour

Cornmeal or grits

Bread or tortillas (store in fridge if not used quickly)

Canned & Jarred Goods

Beans (black, kidney, chickpeas)

Canned tomatoes (diced or crushed)

Tomato paste

Canned tuna or salmon

Peanut butter

Jam or jelly

Baking & Breakfast

Sugar (white or brown)

Baking powder

Baking soda

Vanilla extract

Coffee/tea

Oils & Vinegars

Cooking oil (vegetable or olive oil)

Vinegar (white or cider vinegar)

Soy sauce or hot sauce (optional, but you never know!)

Spices (Just the Essentials)

Salt

Black pepper

Garlic powder

Onion powder

Paprika

Italian seasoning or Cajun blend

Refrigerator Essentials

Focus on fresh basics and things that go with everything.

Proteins & Dairy

Eggs

Cheese (block or shredded)

Deli meat or bacon

Plain yogurt or milk (dairy or nondairy)

Produce

Onions

Garlic

Bell peppers

Carrots

Celery

Lemons or limes

Salad greens or spinach

Other Basics

Butter or margarine

Condiments: ketchup, mustard, mayonnaise

Pickles or relish

Milk (or milk alternative)

Freezer Essentials

Store protein, frozen vegetables, and easy meals.

QUANTITY TIP: If shopping for a family of three or four, I recommend stocking the freezer, because it means you go to the store less often! If single, you can use quart-size freezer bags to break down meats into servings. For example, I'd put four chicken legs in 1-quart bag if I were alone, because that would give me possibly lunch and dinner for two days.

Proteins

Chicken (thighs, breasts, or drumsticks)

Ground beef or turkey

Frozen shrimp or fish

Veggies & Fruit

Frozen mixed vegetables

Frozen spinach or broccoli

Frozen fruit (for smoothies or snacks)

Convenient Must-Haves

Bread (if not eaten fast)

Waffles or pancakes

Cooked rice or grains (for quick reheats)

Leftovers or prepped meals

Kitchen Tools You Actually Need

Skillet (nonstick or cast iron)

Saucepan

Baking sheet

Spatula, spoon, knife, cutting board

Can opener

Measuring cups/spoons

A Fresh Day Should Start with a Clean Kitchen

"The Kitchen should always be neat and clean. The Tables, Pastry Boards, Pans, and everything pertaining to Cookery should be well cleansed."
—Malinda Russell

Malinda's advice was from the hip, matter-of-fact, and spot on. She treated the kitchen just as it is, the heart of the household. Have you ever noticed when your house gets out of hand, it starts with the kitchen? The kitchen gets messy, next comes the bedroom, then the bathroom, and so on. Let me take it a step further; pay attention: When you're having days that feel "all over the place," your home or your car can be untidy at the same time! Our outsides can reflect our inside and moods. In my own home, I've noticed how the mornings go when things are not in order. I tell my kids, "If the kitchen isn't cleaned at night, that means the next day isn't a fresh start, because I'm still standing in yesterday," and it's true.

Talking to someone about cleaning a kitchen may seem like a self-explanatory conversation, but some things we learn as kids, we learn because it's a chore and a "must-do" action, part of earning our keep, in a sense. Fundamentals aren't always taught to let kids know how life can be made easier or the full reason of why we do what we do, so when we become adults, they can slip away from the importance. Also, let's be honest: When we are in a transition period, simple things that we've done every day can be forgotten, and conversations like this can be a reminder of the control we really have over parts of our lives. It's not at all about being perfect; it's about figuring out how we get in our own way and what things can be done about it. Don't be hard on yourself by saying one of the most toxic things we can tell ourselves when we should be giving ourselves compassion: "I should know better." That doesn't help anything. How about: "I see how those things can alter my days and moods; let's take steps toward a better way!" Maybe you're reading this, and you raised yourself, so none of these conversations were had; either way, let's establish some order in the home, starting with the heart of the home: the kitchen.

Once the kitchen is ready, it's time to cook!

PART ONE

YOU GOTTA EAT, RIGHT?

Reading Malinda Russell's story reminded me that food has always been a map for survival. Her recipes show what it meant to create something beautiful in a world that didn't always make room for her. It wasn't just directions for cooking; it was direct evidence of how she lived, stretched, and found ways to care for herself and others.

The more I sat with her story, the more I thought about the elders in my own life. Every conversation about what they used to eat carried wisdom on how to make a little stretch into plenty, how to season when the cupboard was light, how to mark a moment with something sweet even in hard times. What we learn from her and our elders is that food is never just food. It's resilience, memory, and legacy served on a plate. Cooking from that place keeps us rooted, and it reminds us that survival can be delicious and full of dignity.

CHAPTER ONE

RECIPES TO LEARN BY HEART

Historic recipes reflect the language of the times, and Malinda's are often short, written in a commonsense kind of way. It was as if you could tell that the way she wrote was exactly what you needed to hear, before all of today's fancy measuring styles and detailed how-to-style recipes.

It felt like it was shot straight from the hip to the countertop. One could look and think, "How in the world will I be able to make this?" I saw it and knew exactly what tone she had—it's that lovely motherly tone my mama was so good at giving, and that tone is: "This is what you have to do, and this is what you gotta do," no sugar given, just the help she saw you needed.

I love that approach, in many ways of handling things in life. Sometimes, the fluff can prohibit you from getting what you need out of the moment. Now, many need the luxury of the times that we are in, in the most affordable but doable way possible. We want the glam, but we want it with ease and a touch of comfort.

This chapter contains the sort of simple recipes I think everyone should know and have.

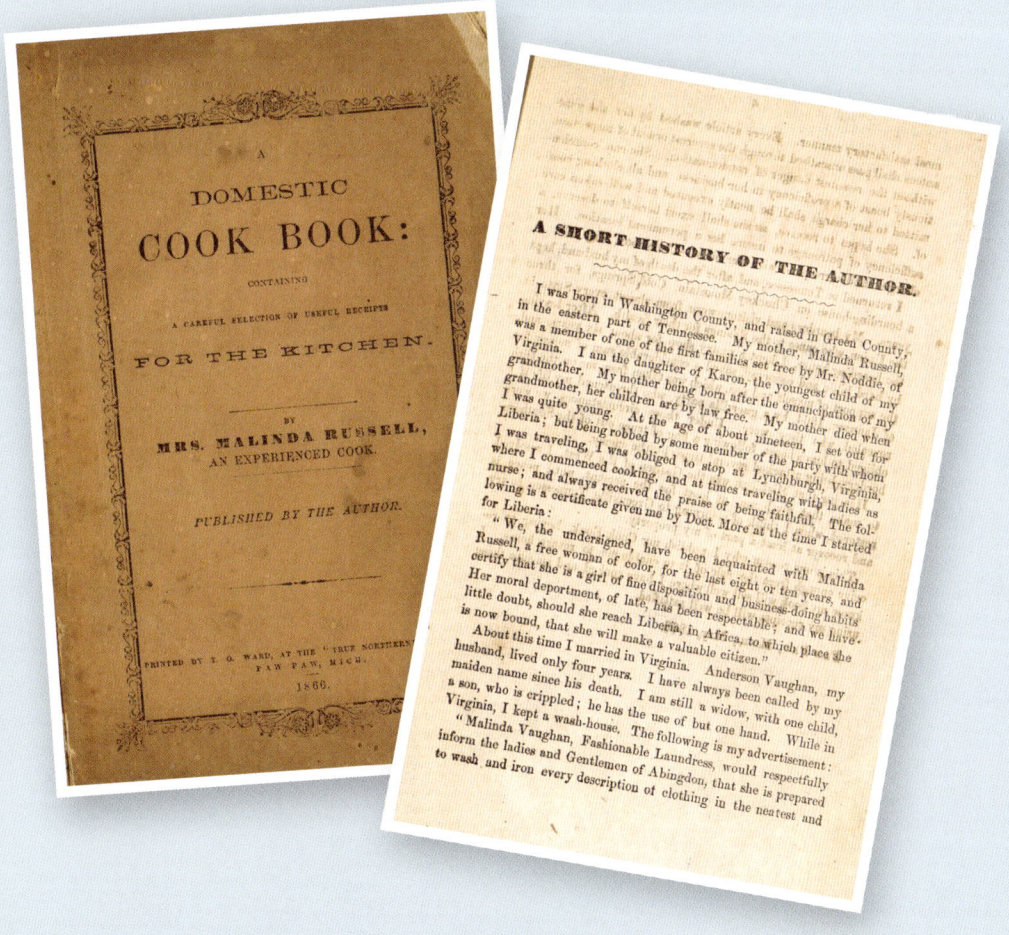

CREAM CRACKERS

MAKES ABOUT 2 DOZEN CRACKERS

Malinda Russell's cream crackers look simple at first glance, but that's what makes them powerful. They speak to the creativity and resourcefulness of her time, by taking just a handful of ingredients and turning them into something delicious. Sometimes, it's in the plain and simple recipes that you find the most joy.

1 quart flour (about 4 cups), plus more for dusting

½ teaspoon salt

4 tablespoons (½ stick) butter, at room temperature, plus more for pan

1 cup fresh cream

1 Preheat the oven to 375°F. Mix the flour and salt together in a bowl. Cut in the butter until the mixture is crumbly, then stir in the cream to form a dough.

2 Roll out the dough on a floured surface until about ¼ inch thick, then cut into squares or rounds. Place on a buttered baking sheet and prick each cracker with a fork.

3 Bake for 12 to 15 minutes, or until lightly golden and crisp. Remove from the oven and let cool before serving.

TRADITIONAL MAC AND CHEESE

SERVES 4 TO 6

Traditional mac and cheese will never let you down. It's the perfect plus-one for your gathering as well. It's a dish that will never grow old and will always be a comfort food to remind you of love and good times. Serve it as a main dish or a side—either way, it's a must-have at your dinner table!

1 pound uncooked elbow macaroni (or pasta of choice)

4 tablespoons (½ stick) butter

4 tablespoons all-purpose flour

4 cups whole milk, warmed

3 cups shredded sharp Cheddar cheese (or a combination: Cheddar + mozzarella + Gouda)

1 teaspoon salt, or to taste

½ teaspoon freshly ground black pepper

½ teaspoon garlic powder (optional)

½ teaspoon smoked paprika (optional)

1 Cook the pasta according to the package directions, then drain and set aside.

2 In a large pot, melt the butter over medium heat and whisk in the flour to form a smooth paste. Slowly pour in the warm milk while whisking constantly, and continue to cook until the sauce thickens and lightly coats the back of a spoon.

3 Stir in the shredded cheese, a handful at a time, until the sauce is smooth and creamy, then season with salt, pepper, and the garlic powder or paprika, if using.

4 Add the cooked pasta to the sauce and stir until every noodle is coated in cheesy goodness.

CHICKEN SOUP

SERVES 4 TO 6

My mama does a good chicken soup, but it's not at all quick. I think it's good to take it slow with some recipes, but with this one, I love the speed. Having pre-cooked tender meat changes the game and makes it so it's no hassle whatsoever!

1 tablespoon oil

1 onion, chopped

3 garlic cloves, minced

2 carrots, sliced

2 celery ribs, sliced

1 bay leaf

6 cups chicken stock

2 cups shredded cooked chicken

Salt and freshly ground black pepper

About 1 cup uncooked noodles (optional)

1 Heat the oil in a large skillet over medium heat, then sauté the onion, garlic, carrots, and celery until softened.

2 Add the bay leaf and chicken stock and bring to a simmer. Add the chicken and cook for 15 to 20 minutes, to blend the flavors.

3 Add the noodles, if using, and cook at a simmer until tender, about 10 minutes. Season to taste.

BEEF SOUP

For healing and "nostalgia in a bowl," I think beef and chicken noodle soups are the best fits! Slow-cooked veggies, tender beef, and a rich broth screams "home"!

1½ pounds beef stew meat or shank, cut into chunks

Salt and freshly ground black pepper

1 tablespoon olive oil

1 onion, chopped

3 garlic cloves, minced

2 carrots, chopped

2 celery ribs, chopped

2 potatoes, cubed

6 cups beef stock

1 bay leaf

1 teaspoon dried thyme

1 Season the beef with salt and pepper. In a large pot over medium-high heat, sear it in the oil until browned on all sides. Remove the beef from the pot and set aside.

2 In the same pot, sauté the onion and garlic until fragrant. Add the carrots, celery, and potatoes; cook for 5 minutes.

3 Return the beef to the pot. Add the stock, bay leaf, and thyme. Simmer for 1½ to 2 hours, until the beef is tender and the broth is rich.

BUTTERMILK ROASTED CHICKEN

SERVES 2 TO 4

You can always count on buttermilk to save any day that includes poultry! If you've ever wondered how you get the juices of the meat to have any flavor, this is the way to go. It's a win!

2 cups buttermilk

1 tablespoon salt

1 teaspoon freshly ground black pepper

1 teaspoon paprika

1 teaspoon garlic powder

½ teaspoon cayenne

1 tablespoon brown sugar

1 whole chicken (3½ to 4 pounds)

1 tablespoon oil or melted butter for roasting

1 In a large bowl or zip-top bag, mix the buttermilk with the salt, black pepper, paprika, garlic powder, cayenne, and brown sugar. Add the chicken and coat it well. Cover and refrigerate overnight (or at least 8 hours), turning once or twice.

2 Preheat the oven to 425°F. Remove the chicken from its marinade, letting the excess drip off. Pat lightly with paper towels—don't rinse. Place the chicken in a roasting pan and brush with oil or butter. Roast for 50 to 70 minutes, depending on size, until the internal temperature reaches 165°F. Remove from the oven and let rest for 10 to 15 minutes before serving.

TIP: If you're serving chicken to a crowd, you can make a variety and put them on a large platter. My firm suggestion is for you to have garlic-buttered Texas toast, naan, pretzel buns, or any breads you think your guests would like; bowls of sauces (bottled sauces are fine); and pickles, shredded cabbage/lettuce, and whatever other toppings you can think of. Let your guests have a grand time eating and building their personal bites!

BBQ ROASTED CHICKEN

SERVES 2 TO 4

BBQ chicken should always include extra sauce and white bread on the side, for a quick sandwich. I think this one and Thai Chile Chicken will be the wow factor of the platter, only because it's not often you see a whole roasted chicken covered in delicious glaze. It's perfection!

1 whole chicken (3½ to 4 pounds)

1 tablespoon oil or melted butter

1 tablespoon liquid smoke (hickory or mesquite)

1 teaspoon salt

½ teaspoon freshly ground black pepper

BBQ SPICE RUB

1 tablespoon brown sugar

2 teaspoons smoked paprika

1 teaspoon garlic powder

1 teaspoon onion powder

½ teaspoon chili powder

½ teaspoon mustard powder

Pinch of cayenne

BBQ GLAZE

½ cup BBQ sauce

1 teaspoon liquid smoke

1 tablespoon cider vinegar or honey

1   Preheat the oven to 400°F. Pat the chicken dry. In a small bowl, mix the oil with the liquid smoke and rub it all over and under the skin.

2   Prepare the BBQ spice rub: In a small bowl, combine the brown sugar, paprika, garlic powder, onion powder, chili powder, mustard powder, and cayenne. Massage it evenly over the chicken.

3   Place the chicken in a roasting pan, breast side up. Roast for 60 to 75 minutes, depending on size, basting once with pan juices.

4   If using the glaze, in a small bowl, stir together the BBQ sauce, liquid smoke, and cider vinegar or honey, and brush it on the chicken during the last 15 minutes of roasting.

5   The chicken is done when its internal temperature reaches 165°F and the juices run clear. Remove from the oven and let rest for 10 to 15 minutes before carving.

THAI CHILE CHICKEN

SERVES 2 TO 4

This is delicious and, honestly, can just be served with basmati rice seasoned with salt and freshly ground black pepper. It's different, and I think it's a great way to keep people stuck to the table talking and eating. Make extra sauce just in case, and if you can keep the juices from the pan, that's even better for dipping!

1 whole chicken (3½ to 4 pounds)

1 tablespoon salt

1 tablespoon oil for rubbing skin

MARINADE

3 tablespoons Thai sweet chili sauce

1½ tablespoons soy sauce

1 tablespoon Asian fish sauce

1 tablespoon honey or brown sugar

1 tablespoon freshly squeezed lime juice

4 garlic cloves, minced

One 1-inch piece fresh ginger, grated

1 to 2 Thai bird chiles, minced (adjust to heat preference)

Zest of 1 lime (optional)

1 Clean and pat the chicken dry. Rub it all over with salt and a bit of oil.

2 Prepare the marinade: In a bowl, mix together the chili sauce, soy sauce, fish sauce, honey, lime juice, garlic, ginger, Thai bird chiles, and lime zest (if using) until well blended. Gently loosen the skin of the chicken and spoon some marinade underneath, then coat the outside thoroughly, reserving some of the unused marinade for basting, if desired. Let marinate for at least 4 hours or overnight, in the fridge.

3 Preheat the oven to 400°F. Place the chicken, breast side up, on a rack in a roasting pan. Roast for 60 to 75 minutes, basting once or twice with the pan juices or reserved marinade, if using. Cover with foil if browning too fast. Remove from the oven and let rest for 10 to 15 minutes before carving.

GARLIC PARMESAN ROASTED CHICKEN

SERVES 2 TO 4

You know me—if it's cooked with a lot of garlic, sign me up twice! It can be done alone or apart from the platter; either way, you can't go wrong. The majority of the room eats chicken at most events! So, you're starting out strong with this one. Sit back and enjoy watching happy bellies and rake in the compliments!

1 whole chicken (3½ to
    4 pounds)

1½ teaspoons salt

½ teaspoon freshly ground
    black pepper

1 tablespoon olive oil

GARLIC BUTTER

6 tablespoons (¾ stick)
    unsalted butter, melted

6 garlic cloves, minced

1 tablespoon freshly squeezed
    lemon juice

1 teaspoon Italian seasoning or
    dried thyme

½ teaspoon crushed red pepper
    flakes (optional)

PARMESAN TOPPING

½ cup finely grated Parmesan
    cheese

1 tablespoon bread crumbs for
    extra crispiness

GARNISH

1 tablespoon chopped fresh
    parsley

1 Preheat the oven to 400°F. Pat the chicken dry, then rub all over with salt, pepper, and olive oil.

2 Prepare the garlic butter: In a small bowl, combine the melted butter, garlic, lemon juice, Italian seasoning, and red pepper flakes, if using. Spoon or brush some of the garlic butter under the skin and all over the outside of the chicken.

3 Roast the chicken, breast side up, in a roasting pan or large oven-proof skillet for 50 to 60 minutes, basting once or twice.

4 Before the last 15 minutes of roasting, mix together the Parmesan and bread crumbs, then sprinkle over the top of the chicken. Continue to roast the chicken until the top is golden and crisp, and the chicken reaches 165°F internal temperature. Remove from the oven and let rest for 10 to 15 minutes.

5 Garnish with fresh parsley before serving.

PASTA CAESAR SALAD

SERVES 4

Oh man, I remember pasta Caesar salad from a box in my first apartment! I thought I was such an adult when I put it in the basket at the store. My favorite part was eating it while it was still warm—oh my gawd. It's one of my faves, so I had to include it. Hold off adding the croutons until you serve each bowl so that, no matter when you eat it, you get the crunch!

8 ounces uncooked short pasta (penne or rotini)

½ cup Caesar dressing

½ cup grated Parmesan cheese

1 cup cherry tomatoes, halved

½ head romaine lettuce, chopped

½ cup croutons

Freshly ground black pepper

1 Cook the pasta in salted water until al dente. Drain and let cool.

2 In a large bowl, toss the pasta with the dressing, Parmesan, tomatoes, and romaine.

3 Top with the croutons and pepper just before serving.

ROAST BEEF

SERVES 6

Malinda believed in mastering the classics, and roast beef is one of them. She was on the right track because the classics all have something valuable in common: They need minimal ingredients, you can feed many by easily multiplying the recipe, and they are damn good and feel like a hug at the end of the day. I think this recipe feels like that, a full-flavored hug. Exactly the type of recipe you need under your belt.

3 to 4 pounds beef roast (chuck, rump, or top round)

2 teaspoons kosher salt

1 teaspoon freshly ground black pepper

1 tablespoon garlic powder

1 tablespoon onion powder or Cajun seasoning

1 tablespoon olive oil or butter

1 medium onion, sliced

3 garlic cloves, smashed

1 tablespoon Worcestershire sauce

1 cup beef broth

4 to 5 medium carrots, cut into large chunks

4 to 5 small potatoes, halved (Yukon Gold or red potatoes work best)

2 to 3 sprigs fresh rosemary or thyme (optional)

1   Preheat the oven to 300°F. Pat the beef roast dry and season it generously with salt, pepper, garlic powder, and onion powder.

2   In a large ovenproof pot or Dutch oven, heat the olive oil over medium-high heat. Sear the roast on all sides until deeply browned, 3 to 4 minutes per side. Add the onion, smashed garlic, Worcestershire sauce, and beef broth to the pot, scraping up any browned bits from the bottom. Arrange the carrots and potatoes around the roast and tuck in the rosemary or thyme, if using.

3   Cover tightly with a lid or foil and put it in the oven to roast for 3½ to 4 hours, basting occasionally, until the beef is very tender and the vegetables are soft.

4   For extra flavor, uncover the pot during the last 20 minutes so the top can brown slightly. Let it rest for 10 minutes before shredding or slicing and remove any chunks of fat before serving.

When starting from scratch, you need community just as much as you need food.

I don't know what my life would look like if I didn't have a village. People often refer to me as resilient and inspiring, but I can only be those things because of the village that nurtures me when I can't nurture myself. It's not just a group of friends, it's intentional lifelines. They give love when it's hard to love yourself, support when you don't have the energy to support yourself, and insight when you can't see past the moment. For some, they're born with that community installed in their family; for others, it's "chosen" family who they've met along the way on their journey, and that's okay! Chosen family are the people that life has allowed you to meet who will be exactly what you thought was missing in your family life. The catch is that you must be open to the blessing. If you sat too long thinking that you were cursed with the lack of community or family love, it may be hard for you to see the blessing trying to get to you, because you're still focusing on the empty space. When, really, you can imagine that empty space as a building that switched locations. It's not where you imagined it would be, but it's waiting somewhere else.

When embracing the idea of community, you must first embrace yourself fully. Be honest about your love languages and needs, and that honesty and level of self-awareness will attract those people to you. I don't recommend trying to get everything from one person, because that can be a lot of pressure. I recommend that you build a tool belt of bonds. You know how you have a hammer, pliers, wrench etc.? Think of that, but with emotional and intellectual attributes. For example, in my community, I have someone I can dream big with, talk business, hash out relationship/family issues with, break down and discuss spiritual topics, life lessons, and the overall tone of my community with transparency. Think deeply about what you need and about what you are willing to be to someone else. It must be a two-way street, especially if you want it to last.

Community bonds must be nurtured in the ways that fit their dynamics. For example, with my community, we do not hold unrealistic expectations at all! We all have busy lives, so we aren't hanging out or calling too often—but we show up and out for one another! Personally, I'm not a big quality-time person when it comes to friendships, but I will answer the phone at two a.m. if someone needs it, spend hours talking them through something, feed them, or show up in those sacred moments—and they accept me fully. I really believe reciprocity is the key to any thriving community. When reciprocity is present, you have the perfect balance.

TRADITIONAL POTATO SALAD

SERVES 6

Potato salad seems like a simple thing, maybe even a side people have that doesn't count for much, like a filler. But in the Black culture, it's a defining moment. Who made the potato salad? Is it sweet? Or tangy? What color is it, yellow or pale? Yes, all these questions are asked because, culturally, every side dish counts and potato salad tends to carry a grandmother's love with each spoonful. Here's a recipe that will get you through critique! My suggestion would be, don't be afraid of salt and a little cayenne if you're brave!

3 pounds russet or Yukon Gold potatoes

1 cup mayonnaise

2 tablespoons prepared yellow mustard

½ cup sweet pickle relish (or chopped dill pickles, if you prefer less sweet)

½ cup finely chopped celery

½ cup finely chopped onion

1 tablespoon pickle juice (optional)

4 hard-boiled eggs (3 chopped, 1 sliced for garnish)

Salt and freshly ground black (or cayenne) pepper

Paprika for garnish

1 Peel and dice the potatoes into chunks, then place them in a large pot of salted water. Boil until fork-tender, then drain and let cool slightly.

2 In a large bowl, combine the mayonnaise, mustard, relish, celery, onion, and pickle juice, if using. Gently fold in the potatoes, along with the chopped eggs, mixing until everything is coated but still a little chunky. Taste and season with salt and pepper.

3 Transfer to a serving dish, top with a sliced hard-boiled egg and a light dusting of paprika, then chill for at least an hour before serving, so the flavors come together.

GARLIC MASHED POTATOES

SERVES 4 TO 6

In my humble opinion, I think that if it's chunky potatoes in the mashed potatoes, you must love me because the chunks give it a gourmet touch! Having a good, mashed potatoes recipe under your belt is third in line after mac and cheese and potato salad. It's always a good time for mashed potatoes. Keep this recipe in mind when you need a side for chicken fried or roasted, but it's gonna kill with the Salisbury steak or even eaten stand-alone, loaded with your favorite toppings!

2 pounds Yukon Gold or russet potatoes, peeled and cubed

5 to 7 garlic cloves, peeled

4 tablespoons (½ stick) butter

½ cup milk or cream, warmed

Salt and freshly ground black pepper

Fresh parsley for garnish

1 Boil the potatoes and garlic in salted water until tender, about 15 minutes.

2 Drain, then mash with the butter and warm milk. Season to taste with salt and pepper, and garnish with fresh parsley.

CONGRI

SERVES 4 TO 6

I can eat beans and rice any way they are served! I come from New Orleans where red beans is one of our food babies, so congri was a match made in heaven for me. I love the way Cubans build flavor for their dishes and still give space for flexibility. Plus, congri can be eaten alone or as a side for any protein (try it with Cuban Pork, page 79). It's comforting and filling at the same time.

1 cup dried black beans (or one 15-ounce can, drained and rinsed)

2 tablespoons olive oil or pork fat

1 small onion, finely chopped

1 green bell pepper, finely chopped

3 garlic cloves, minced

1 teaspoon ground cumin

½ teaspoon dried oregano

½ teaspoon smoked paprika

1 bay leaf

2 cups long-grain white rice

3 cups water or bean cooking liquid (or a combination)

1½ teaspoon salt (adjust to taste)

Fresh cilantro or parsley for garnish (optional)

1 If using dried beans, soak them overnight, then drain and cook in fresh water until just tender, 45 to 60 minutes; reserve 2 to 3 cups of the cooking liquid. If using canned beans, skip this step.

2 In a large pot or deep skillet, heat the olive oil over medium heat. Add the onion, bell pepper, and garlic and sauté until softened and fragrant. Stir in the cumin, oregano, smoked paprika, and bay leaf, letting them simmer for a few seconds.

3 Add the rice and stir to coat each grain. Pour in the beans and their cooking liquid (or water), season with salt, and stir well to combine.

4 Bring the mixture to a boil, then reduce the heat to low, cover, and simmer for about 20 minutes, or until the rice is tender and has absorbed the liquid.

5 Remove from the heat and let it rest, covered, for 5 minutes. Serve with fresh cilantro or parsley as a garnish.

HOMESTYLE WHITE BEANS

SERVES 4 TO 6

I'm a bean-any-way-you-cook-them type of girl, and I'm a sucker for a good pot of white beans. For some reason, I don't want fried chicken with white beans; I want baked chicken or ham. It just feels like the right thing to do. To me, white beans have a smoother and softer taste, almost heartwarming. You can eat them with rice, but recently, I cooked and ate them alone in a bowl when it was cold outside. My advice would be to fill a quart-size freezer bag with cooked beans, and freeze it for a go-to meal in the future.

1 pound dried white beans

2 tablespoons olive oil or bacon drippings

1 smoked sausage or ham hock

1 onion, chopped

1 bell pepper, chopped

1 celery rib, chopped

3 garlic cloves, minced

1 teaspoon dried thyme

1 bay leaf

9 cups water or broth

Salt and freshly ground black pepper

1   Soak the beans overnight, or use the quick-soak method.

2   Heat the oil or drippings in a large pot over medium-high heat and sauté the sausage until sticky, then transfer it to a plate, leaving the sausage fat in the pan. Add the onion, bell pepper, celery, and garlic and sauté until soft.

3   Add the soaked beans, thyme, bay leaf, and water or broth. Bring to a boil.

4   Lower the heat and simmer for 1½ to 2 hours, until the beans are tender and the broth is creamy. Add the sausage at the 1½-hour point. Adjust the seasoning.

TIP: Remember the beans need to be a little salty when you taste them by themselves, because, if they aren't, when you mix them with the rice, the mixture will taste bland. It's why I say, "Rice can embarrass you," when it erases all of your hard work seasoning the beans.

MARINATED BEAN SALAD

SERVES 4 TO 6

Please put this on the "affordable potluck" list! Often in my tightest times, when I worked in an office setting, we had potluck moments that made me cringe because I couldn't afford it. Truthfully, I would aim to find something that was low budget but presented in a fancy way. The secret to getting away with canned items is the power that comes with rinsing off canned veggies or beans. It removes that canned taste and then you can just enjoy the food without worrying about feeling a touch too frugal. Once you make this, all you can taste is the flavor!

½ cup olive oil

2 tablespoons red wine vinegar

1 teaspoon Dijon mustard

5 to 7 garlic cloves, minced

Salt and freshly ground black pepper

One 14-ounce can kidney beans, drained

One 14-ounce can cannellini or navy beans, drained

One 14-ounce can chickpeas, drained

½ red onion, sliced thinly

1 celery stalk, sliced thinly

½ cup chopped fresh parsley

1 Whisk together the oil, red wine vinegar, mustard, garlic, salt, and pepper in a large bowl.

2 Add the kidney beans, cannellini beans, chickpeas, red onion, celery, and parsley. Toss to coat.

3 Marinate for at least 1 hour in the fridge before serving.

SWEET MILK MUFFINS

MAKES 12 MUFFINS

Malinda had this listed in her cookbook, so I thought, while I was making muffins, that it was only right to include an updated version! It's a good partner in crime for a cup of coffee. Not too sweet, it's a muffin that will calm a craving but not make you feel guilty for the sugar. A very mellow and sophisticated taste with a vintage flair. I'm not gonna lie—it felt as if I was time traveling, tasting what they were into back then; it was a good feeling. I enjoyed it and I hope you do, too. See photograph on page 90.

1½ cups all-purpose flour

½ cup sugar

2 teaspoons baking powder

½ teaspoon salt

⅔ cup sweetened condensed milk

⅓ cup (5 tablespoons + 1 teaspoon) butter, melted

1 large egg

1 teaspoon pure vanilla extract

1 Preheat the oven to 375°F and line a standard 12-muffin tin with paper liners.

2 Mix together the flour, sugar, baking powder, and salt in a large bowl.

3 In a small bowl, combine the condensed milk, butter, egg, and vanilla.

4 Stir the milk mixture into the flour mixture.

5 Spoon into the prepared muffin tin. Bake for 18 to 20 minutes.

PLAIN CAKE

SERVES 6 TO 8

Malinda Russell wrote down a recipe for plain cake back in 1866, when she was the first known Black woman to publish a cookbook in this country. What I love about it is how it's just the basics, but still full of meaning. When I bake this cake, I think of how she didn't just write recipes, she left a piece of herself in those pages. It reminds me that even the simplest cake can carry a story and a whole lot of history with it.

1 cup (2 sticks) unsalted butter, at room temperature, plus more for pan

3 cups sugar

6 large eggs

1 teaspoon baking soda

1 cup sour milk or buttermilk

3 cups all-purpose flour

1 teaspoon cream of tartar

Freshly squeezed lemon juice and zest (optional)

1 Preheat the oven to 325°F and generously butter a 9-inch Bundt or angel cake pan.

2 In a large bowl, cream together the butter and sugar until light and fluffy. Beat in the eggs, one at a time, until the mixture is smooth. In a separate bowl, stir the baking soda into the sour milk. Sift together the flour and cream of tartar onto a sheet of wax paper or into another bowl. Add the flour mixture and sour milk alternately to the creamed mixture, starting and ending with the flour. Stir just until everything is combined. If you'd like, fold in a splash of lemon juice and a little zest, for brightness. Pour the batter into your prepared pan and smooth the top.

3 Bake until golden and a toothpick inserted into the center comes out clean—about an hour.

4 Remove from the oven and let the cake cool before slicing.

CHAPTER TWO

RECIPES THAT FEEL LIKE HOME TO ME

As my parents believed, cooking wasn't some gender thing, it was a human thing. So, it's incredibly important to find your spot in the food game. Maybe you do it all, maybe you prep, maybe you grocery shop, maybe you clean up, or maybe—just maybe—you're the one who occasionally buys dinner to make the night go smoothly. Find your part, and know that chances are you'll be playing all roles at some point.

This set of recipes are some that have held my hand and comforted me throughout changes in my life. Some stuff is from my home, New Orleans, but as you know, New Orleans is a melting pot; the food of the locals wasn't the only food that cradled me through times of rebuilding, transitioning, or starting over. You'll find influences from my home, Cuban culture, African, Jamaican, French, and a touch of German and Japanese. Some of these meals were hugs when I needed it or a friend to share a moment of success with. These meals are a mixture of comfort and cultural staples to have under your belt.

I suggest finding any way you can to incorporate culture into your lifestyle, apart from the clothes you wear, shows you watch, or music you listen to—there's more. Meals are a lot like a conversation waiting to happen. A bird's-eye view into someone's way of living. It's a very good practice to think of the lives of others with curiosity and consideration. It's a brilliant way to work out the "being a good human" muscle: by eating the food, thinking about flavors you've never tasted before or the ones that are similar. It's actually fun!

Listen, I have a thing I say to friends when it comes to food: "If I'm gonna consume the calories, it's gotta be well seasoned and worth it." Let's stretch ourselves—let's eat good food and try something new.

AFRICAN SPINACH STEW

SERVES 4

Spinach is a sign of strength, resourcefulness, and its connection to earth. It's a humble and grounding meal that can heal the body as well. All those things you need when starting over from any point; in fact, it's one of your greatest needs! I cooked this and I immediately thought of my daddy; the bold flavors go perfectly with smoked meats. I sent him a container and he immediately called and said how he loved it and how the flavor was crazy! It's such a well-seasoned, balanced dish, you can combine it with rice or eat it with Fufu (page 53).

2 tablespoons palm oil

1 onion, chopped

4 garlic cloves, minced

1 tablespoon grated fresh ginger

1 bell pepper, diced

1 tomato, chopped

1 teaspoon paprika

1 teaspoon bouillon powder or seasoning salt

¼ teaspoon cayenne (optional)

2 cups cooked protein (beef, chicken, or fish)

1 pound fresh spinach, or one 16-ounce package frozen, thawed and drained

1 Heat the oil in a large, deep skillet over medium heat.

2 Sauté the onion until golden. Add the garlic, ginger, and bell pepper; cook until softened.

3 Stir in the tomato, paprika, bouillon powder, and cayenne. Simmer until thickened.

4 Add the protein and spinach. Stir and simmer for 10 to 15 minutes, until the stew is rich and flavorful.

POULET YASSA

SERVES 4 TO 6

The tanginess drew me in, and the tenderness of the chicken won me over. Cooking African meals is an honor, because while all cooking feels like communication, for me as an African-American, it feels like a language of homage and respect. It feels right. I think of Malinda Russell and her dream of returning to Africa. She never made that journey, but dishes like poulet yassa carry that longing, that connection across water. When I cook it, I feel part of that same bridge reaching back with gratitude and carrying it forward with love.

2 pounds chicken thighs or legs

¼ cup freshly squeezed lemon juice

¼ cup Dijon mustard

4 garlic cloves, minced

Salt and freshly ground black pepper

3 onions, sliced thinly

2 tablespoons olive oil

1 Scotch bonnet pepper

1   Marinate the chicken in the lemon juice, Dijon mustard, garlic, salt, and pepper for at least 1 hour or overnight. Place the sliced onions in the marinade, too.

2   Heat the oil in a large skillet over medium heat. Remove the chicken from the marinade and sear until golden and crisped. Set aside.

3   In the same pan, sauté the onion from the marinade until soft and golden. Return the chicken to the pan along with all of its marinade. Add the scotch bonnet, cover, and simmer over medium heat for 40 to 45 minutes, until tender with a rich tangy-sweet sauce.

FUFU

SERVES 4

What I love about fufu isn't just the food itself, but the way it's eaten. In many African cultures, eating with your hands is a sign of connection to the earth, to the meal, and to the people around you. There's something powerful about tearing off a piece of fufu, dipping it into soup, and sharing that same rhythm with everyone at the table. It's communal, it's grounding, and it reminds me that food isn't just about flavor, it's about fellowship.

4 cups water

Pinch of salt (optional)

2 cups cassava flour, plantain flour, or yam flour

1 Bring the water to a boil in a large, nonstick pot and add a pinch of salt, if you'd like. Slowly sprinkle in the cassava flour while whisking constantly so it doesn't clump. Once all the flour is in, lower the heat to medium and keep stirring vigorously with a wooden spoon until the mixture becomes smooth, stretchy, and thick, 5 to 10 minutes. Cover the pot and let the fufu steam gently over low heat for another 2 to 3 minutes, so it firms up.

2 When it's ready, shape the fufu into round portions and serve it warm. Traditionally, you tear off a piece with your fingers, press it gently, and dip it into a flavorful soup or stew, so it soaks up the seasoning.

FRENCH ONION SOUP

SERVES 4 TO 6

It doesn't get any classier than this. . . . Man, I remember preparing packet after packet of those Lipton French onion soup mixes in the 1990s, thinking I had sophisticated taste. Well, I'm all grown now, and I can make a damn good French onion soup that'll make you put your pinkie out! Cooking the onions down is the hardest part because you'll want to eat them out of the pan! I love the toast on top because it's just edible drama, but what if . . . maybe . . . you made a grilled cheese with garlic butter to dip in the soup instead? Don't shoot the messenger; I'll drop a grilled cheese recipe at the end.

2 tablespoons butter

1 tablespoon olive oil

4 large onions, sliced thinly

½ teaspoon salt

1 teaspoon sugar

2 garlic cloves, minced

½ cup dry white wine or additional beef stock

4 cups beef stock

1 teaspoon dried thyme

1 bay leaf

TO SERVE
Toasted baguette slices

Grated Gruyère or Swiss cheese

Microgreens

1   Melt together the butter and oil in a large pot. Add the onions, salt, and sugar. Cook over medium heat for 30 to 40 minutes, stirring often, until deeply caramelized.

2   Stir in the garlic and cook for 1 minute. Deglaze with the wine, scraping up the brown bits.

3   Add the beef stock, thyme, and bay leaf. Simmer for 20 minutes.

4   Serve hot with toasted baguette slices, topped with melted cheese and microgreens for serving.

GARLIC BUTTER GRILLED CHEESE

SERVES 1 OR 2

Depending on the rest of the menu for the night, I'd suggest allocating half a sandwich per person when accompanied by a big bowl of hearty soup, but if it's the full dinner, multiply the recipe as needed and carry on with a good night! It's an elegant spin on a cozy classic and it's gonna be damn good when you dip the sourdough bread into soup!

2 slices sourdough bread

1 tablespoon garlic butter, at room temperature

1 teaspoon mayonnaise

1 slice Gruyère cheese

1 slice Swiss cheese

1 Spread the garlic butter on one side of both bread slices.

2 Spread the mayonnaise on the other side of one or both bread slices.

3 Layer the Gruyère and Swiss cheese between the bread slices, mayo sides facing in.

4 Heat a skillet over medium heat. Place a sandwich in the skillet and cook until golden brown and the cheese is melted, 3 to 4 minutes per side, pressing gently with a spatula for an even crisp.

TIP: Use a lid while cooking to help melt the cheese faster.

JAMAICAN CURRY

SERVES 4 TO 6

In my opinion, our daddy makes the best curry—whether it's chicken or veggies, it's always killer. Curry is one of the best meals to add to an anti-inflammatory diet. You can adjust the curry as you please and even add turmeric. It's a great meal that's flavorful with a purpose, and also, I just love curry! It could be Jamaican or Thai—if it's on the menu, I'm getting it. I hope you enjoy it and switch it up! I'm not gonna lie: It's amazing with just tomatoes!

2 pounds bone-in or boneless chicken thighs

4 tablespoons Jamaican curry powder, plus a pinch for pot

1 teaspoon allspice

1 teaspoon dried hyme

1 teaspoon salt, plus more to taste

½ teaspoon freshly ground black pepper

2 tablespoons olive oil

1 onion, chopped

4 garlic cloves, minced

2 cups diced potatoes

1 Scotch bonnet pepper, whole or chopped (optional)

½ cup water or chicken stock

Cooked rice for serving

1 Rub the chicken with the curry powder, allspice, thyme, 1 teaspoon of salt, and the black pepper. In the fridge, let marinate for 1 hour or overnight to deepen flavor.

2 Heat the oil over medium-high heat in a large, heavy pot. Add a pinch of curry powder to toast in the oil, then sear the chicken on both sides until browned. Remove from the pot and set aside.

3 In the same pot, sauté the onion and garlic until golden and fragrant. Add the potatoes and Scotch bonnet and return the chicken to the pot. Add the water or stock. Simmer, covered, for 35 to 40 minutes, allowing the curry to thicken and flavor the chicken throughout. Serve with rice.

RED THAI CURRY SOUP

SERVES 4

Soups can go from being in a homestyle category to a white tablecloth lane with just a few ingredients. Even though this will be done at home, it definitely has a white tablecloth feel and taste. I thoroughly enjoy this soup; once you taste it you also will, and once you serve it, everyone else will, too!

1 tablespoon coconut or vegetable oil

2 to 3 tablespoons red Thai curry paste (adjust to taste)

3 cloves garlic, minced

1-inch piece fresh ginger, grated

1 small onion, sliced

1 red bell pepper, sliced

1 small zucchini or carrot, sliced (optional)

One 14-ounce can coconut milk

3 cups vegetable or chicken broth

1 tablespoon fish sauce (or soy sauce for vegetarian)

1 tablespoon lime juice

1 teaspoon brown sugar (optional)

1 to 2 cups protein of choice: tofu, shrimp, chicken, or mushrooms (optional)

Cooked jasmine rice or rice noodles, for serving (optional)

Fresh basil or cilantro for garnish

1 Heat the coconut oil in a large pot over medium heat. Add the curry paste and stir for about 30 seconds or until fragrant. Stir in the garlic, ginger, and onion and cook until softened. Add the bell pepper and any other vegetables you're using, then pour in the coconut milk and broth.

2 Bring the soup to a gentle simmer and add fish sauce, lime juice, and brown sugar, if desired (it balances the spice), adjusting to taste.

3 Now is the time to add proteins: If using chicken or shrimp, simmer until cooked through; if using tofu or mushrooms, let them soak up the flavors for a few minutes.

4 Serve with jasmine rice or rice noodles, if desired, or just the broth alone can be perfect as well! Garnish with fresh basil or cilantro.

OYSTER STEW

SERVES 4 TO 6

In New Orleans, we don't have seasons—it's either hot summer, not so hot, and cold. That being said, we don't follow rules—we eat hot soups, stews, and bisques when we feel like it, and this is one of them. Oysters are a big thing here, so obviously I had to include an oyster recipe for you to have under your belt. It has a rich and full-bodied flavor that's totally flexible!! You can swap out the oysters to be sautéed portobello mushrooms for a cost-friendly switch. Serve with some garlic bread, and you have a full belly and a good nap on your hands!

2 tablespoons butter

1 small onion, chopped finely

2 garlic cloves, minced

1 pint shucked oysters with their liquor (if using mushrooms, about ¼ cup white wine will do as a substitute)

2 cups whole milk

½ cup heavy whipping cream

Salt and freshly ground black pepper

Cajun seasoning

Pinch of cayenne or paprika

Chopped fresh parsley and lemon wedges for garnish

1 Melt the butter in a large saucepan. Sauté the onion over medium heat until translucent, then add the garlic and cook for 1 more minute. Pour in the oyster liquor and bring to a simmer.

2 Add the oysters and cook just until they begin to curl (2 to 3 minutes). Stir in the milk and cream. Season to taste with salt, pepper, Cajun seasoning, and cayenne. Heat gently—do not boil.

3 Serve hot, garnished with fresh parsley and lemon wedges.

VEGETABLE PHO

SERVES 4

Pho feels like a big sigh of relief. After trying to find that same restaurant I got the amazing bowl of pho from for a few years, I started making my own. So much goes into that liquid—the charring of the veggies builds a tremendous flavor, and the aromatics prove that you don't have to be large to be mighty! The cloves and anise really lock in the flavor in an impressive way. Don't be afraid to get creative with the toppings. Make it good to you, make it your own.

BROTH

1 large onion, halved

One 3-inch piece fresh ginger, halved

4 cups vegetable stock

4 cups water

1 cinnamon stick

2 star anise

4 whole cloves

1 tablespoon soy sauce

1 tablespoon brown sugar

Salt

FOR ASSEMBLY

8 ounces uncooked rice noodles

4 mini bok choy, halved lengthwise

1 cup mushrooms (shiitake or cremini), sliced

1 cup shredded carrot

1 jalapeño pepper, sliced thinly

Fresh cilantro and Thai basil

Lime wedges

1 Make the broth: In a large, dry pot over medium heat, char the onion and ginger, cut side down, until darkened, 4 to 5 minutes.

2 Add the stock, water, cinnamon stick, star anise, cloves, soy sauce, and brown sugar. Season with salt. Bring to a boil, then simmer, uncovered, for 30 minutes. Strain and keep warm. Separately, boil the noodles according to their package instructions. Drain and rinse.

3 For the bowls: In a separate pot, blanch the bok choy and mushrooms in boiling water for 1 to 2 minutes, until just tender.

4 To serve: Divide the cooked noodles among four bowls. Top with the blanched bok choy mushrooms, shredded carrot, and jalapeño slices. Ladle the hot, strained broth over each bowl. Garnish with your fresh herbs and serve with lime wedges.

RAMEN

SERVES 2 TO 4

I started out making ramen at home for my family. Doctoring up packets of Top Ramen on a weeknight was one of my quarantine specialties, but I got curious about a richer taste and decided to make it this way. You can totally make it veggie, vegan, seafood, or meat. Get creative and enjoy an amazing bowl of ramen at home!

1 tablespoon sesame oil or neutral oil

2 garlic cloves, minced

One 1-inch piece ginger, grated

4 cups chicken or veggie stock

2 tablespoons soy sauce

1 tablespoon miso paste (optional)

1 tablespoon rice vinegar

2 individual packets ramen noodles (discard their seasoning)

Toppings: soft-boiled egg, scallions, chili oil, greens, mushrooms

1 Heat the oil in a large pot over medium heat. Sauté the garlic and ginger until fragrant.

2 Add the stock, soy sauce, miso (if using), and rice vinegar. Simmer for 10 minutes to develop the flavor.

3 Cook the ramen noodles separately, according to the package directions, then add to the broth. Ladle into bowls and top as desired.

MINI CRAWFISH PIES

SERVES 6

In New Orleans, there's nothing more exciting than walking up to the food table and seeing mini crawfish pies! It's a homestyle New Orleans delicacy: crawfish with a creamy light gravy, sautéed seasonings, and a buttered crust. It's the best three to four bites of YO LIFE. I think the mini pies are the best bet, because you get the most servings and you get to freeze them if you make too many! Pop them in the oven to reheat, and joy is born again!

1 tablespoon butter

½ cup chopped onion

¼ cup chopped bell pepper

¼ cup chopped celery

2 garlic cloves, minced

1 tablespoon all-purpose flour

½ cup heavy cream or half-and-half

1 teaspoon Creole seasoning

8 ounces crawfish tails (with fat, if available)

Salt and freshly ground black pepper

12 premade frozen or refrigerated mini pie shells (unbaked)

1 large egg, beaten (for egg wash)

Garlic butter, for brushing crusts after baking (optional)

1 Preheat the oven to 375°F.

2 In a large skillet, melt the butter over medium heat. Sauté the onion, bell pepper, celery, and garlic until softened, 5 to 7 minutes. Stir in the flour and cook for 1 minute. Slowly add the cream, stirring until thickened, 1 to 2 minutes. Add the Creole seasoning, crawfish tails, and salt and black pepper. Simmer for 2 to 3 minutes. Remove from the heat and let cool slightly. Spoon the cooled crawfish mixture evenly into the premade mini pie shells. Do not overfill. Brush the edges or tops lightly with the beaten egg for color. Bake on a parchment-lined baking sheet for 18 to 22 minutes, or until golden brown.

3 Brush the warm crusts with garlic butter just before serving, if desired for extra flavor.

GARLIC-LOVERS' CHICKEN POTPIE

SERVES 4

Let me tell you something: Our mama was a chicken noodle soup-from-scratch kinda gal, so a guilty pleasure of mine while growing up was canned soup. I guess it was because I knew that other families ate soup from a can and it felt like a new land to me somehow. Well, that canned soup made me explore chicken potpies! We didn't grow up eating that at all. But man, that was something my daddy and I had in common; we both liked that heartwarming fullness that chicken potpie provided. The flavor feels like a blanket to me, it's so good! Don't talk about if you use meat from a smoked chicken?! My lawd! It's a winner.

Oil for skillet

½ cup diced onion

4 garlic cloves, minced (or more if you love it!)

2 cups cooked chicken (shredded or chopped)

1 cup frozen peas and carrots

One 10.5-ounce can cream of chicken soup

½ cup milk or half-and-half

½ teaspoon garlic powder

½ teaspoon dried thyme or Italian seasoning

Salt and freshly ground black pepper

1 to 2 refrigerated piecrusts

1 Preheat the oven to 400°F.

2 In a small skillet over medium heat, sauté the onion and garlic in a little oil until soft and fragrant, 2 to 3 minutes.

3 In a bowl, mix together the cooked chicken, sautéed garlic and onion, peas and carrots, cream of chicken soup, milk, garlic powder, thyme, and salt and pepper to taste. Taste the mixture to make sure the flavor is slapping.

4 Line a pie dish with one refrigerated crust, add the filling, and top with the second crust (if using). Seal the edges and cut slits in the top.

5 Bake for 30 to 35 minutes, until golden. Remove from the oven and let rest for 5 to 10 minutes before cutting.

SALISBURY STEAK

SERVES 4

I can remember back to my pregnancy with my son Emmanuel, when I would have cravings in the middle of the night, and guess what it would be? Frozen Salisbury steak and mashed potato meals!! Crazy, I know, right? I would buy a gang of them and, every night, wake up half sleepwalking to the microwave to heat up a frozen dinner, add a little Cajun seasoning on top, and gobble it down and go right back to bed. Now that I'm out of that bizarre world of pregnancy cravings, the craving is elevated more toward Salisbury steak and our mama's tender meatloaf. I love to cook with lots of garlic like I'm fending off vampires by night, so a slapping garlic mash has to be included. Our mama makes her meatloaf by adding a little milk for tenderness, like layer cake tender. So, that's what I wanted from my Salisbury steak. Combine that with the gravy and garlic mash, and it'll rock you to sleep!

1 pound ground beef

⅓ cup bread crumbs

¼ cup milk

1 large egg

1 tablespoon Worcestershire sauce

1 teaspoon garlic powder

½ teaspoon onion powder

Salt and freshly ground black pepper

1 tablespoon oil or butter for searing

GRAVY

1 tablespoon butter

½ onion, sliced thinly

2 garlic cloves, minced

2 tablespoons all-purpose flour (or a cornstarch slurry)

2 cups beef stock

1 tablespoon Worcestershire sauce

1 tablespoon ketchup

1 In a bowl, combine the beef, bread crumbs, milk, egg, Worcestershire, garlic powder, onion powder, and salt and pepper. Shape into four patties.

2 Heat the oil in a large skillet over medium-high heat, then brown the patties, 3 to 4 minutes per side. Remove from the pan and set aside.

3 Make the gravy: In the same pan, heat the butter over medium-high heat and sauté the onion and garlic. Stir in the flour and cook for 1 minute. Add the stock, Worcestershire, and ketchup. Simmer until thick.

4 Return the patties to the skillet, placing them in the gravy. Cover and simmer for 10 to 15 minutes, until cooked through.

Life Transitions with Children

Age does not matter at all. My oldest is 26, and my youngest is 7 years old, and trust me, transitions still affect them, even if they aren't in the home. It can feel discouraging hearing that, but perk up! It will mold them and strengthen their mental toughness—and give them the tools to handle change. That's what it all boils down to: change. Children have to be shown it's okay and that, sometimes, it's not fun.

I used to be the kind of parent who would hide fear, tears, and sadness if they angered me in a particular way. Until I realized how I was robbing them from knowing what their actions and reactions can do to others. Imagine never knowing that you giving someone the silent treatment can make them sad or depressed, then one day in the real world you see someone crumble from the same thing. Imagine never seeing fear at home and feeling fear for yourself away from home. Or imagine never seeing someone follow a dream and then discovering your own dream. It would be scary, and in some instances, it would feel like the world is against you, you weren't strong enough, or maybe not bold enough to pull it off. I've learned they need to see as much as they can to harvest those things for lessons.

The same with change: They need to see all the parts of transitions and the roller coaster of emotions that comes with it. The best part is that the respect they have for you later is the real gift. It's a glorious opportunity for them to meet you as a person, not just a mom or a dad. They get to see that you aren't that different from them, that you're just figuring it out as you go too! It's so beautiful when you think of it that way. One of the things that makes kids pull away is that they think their parents have it all together and that it may take them forever to catch up, when that's not the case.

When you let your children see all transitions, at the right time, you will be seen as relatable and wise. They'll have understanding and empathy toward you in the same areas where they used to point fingers. How do you think I know? I have lived it, and I was humble enough to tuck my tail and say, "Ma, thank you and you were right about it all." How did I get there? I would ask questions the same way I would ask a friend questions, about things my mama went through, wanting to know how she felt, what she thought, and how she processed it all. She answered honestly because she could feel she wasn't being judged, she was being seen.

Once I got to know her feelings of anger, fear, or happiness, I started to see everything I'd seen from her over the years with a different light of gratitude. It made me softer toward her and her choices. So, if that transparency can offer that restoration for someone after decades, think about the inner work it tackles in the now, if we are transparent with our kids. Let's face it, they will be discouraged, but will know that it's part of the cycle of life. By being transparent, you aren't exposing yourself to your children, you're revealing yourself to them. You're showing them you trust them, and the bond is important enough to have vulnerability at the table. They will be able to say the same thing I say about my parents: They were real, resilient, and made sure we were prepared for life!

OXTAILS

SERVES 4 TO 6

Oxtails are one of those dishes that feel like home, no matter where you are. In New Orleans, we've always shared a kinship with the Caribbean, from how we season our food to the way we gather around the table. Both cultures know how to take something humble and turn it into a pot of richness that feeds body and soul. That's why oxtails speak to me: They carry the slow-simmered comfort of the Caribbean and the familiar rhythm of New Orleans kitchens, where flavor is stretched, deepened, and shared. Cooking them feels like honoring two branches of the same family tree.

3 to 4 pounds oxtails

Salt and freshly ground black
    pepper

2 tablespoons olive oil

1 onion, chopped

4 garlic cloves, minced

2 tablespoons tomato paste

2 teaspoons browning sauce

1 tablespoon Worcestershire
    sauce

1 teaspoon dried thyme

1 teaspoon allspice

3 cups beef stock

One 14-ounce can butter beans
    (optional)

1 Make sure to trim off as much fat as you can from the oxtails. Season the oxtails well with salt and black pepper. In a large skillet over medium-high heat, sear the oxtails in the oil until deeply browned on all sides. Remove from the pan, leaving the drippings in the pan.

2 In the same skillet, sauté the onion in the drippings until caramelized. Add the garlic, tomato paste, browning sauce, Worcestershire, thyme, and allspice. Stir until the paste darkens and the mixture is fragrant.

3 Return the oxtails to the skillet. Deglaze with a splash of the stock, scraping up the browned bits. Add the remaining stock and simmer, covered, for 2½ to 3 hours, stirring in the butter beans, if using, in the final 20 minutes.

MOLE ENCHILADAS

SERVES 4

Mole enchiladas remind me how powerful it is to step into another culture's kitchen with respect. The richness of the sauce, spices, sweetness, and depth are proof that food is a story written over centuries. As an African-American cook, making mole feels like an embrace, a way of saying, "I see you, I honor your traditions, and I'm grateful for the chance to taste your history." Cooking dishes outside my own roots is a practice in humility and appreciation—a reminder that food is one of the most beautiful bridges we have between people.

MOLE SAUCE

2 dried ancho chiles, stemmed and seeded

2 dried guajillo chiles, stemmed and seeded

2 dried pasilla chiles, stemmed and seeded

2 tablespoons vegetable oil

½ onion chopped

3 garlic cloves

¼ cup raw almonds

2 tablespoons sesame seeds

1 corn tortilla, torn into pieces

1 slice stale bread, torn

1 medium tomato, chopped

1 tablespoon raisins

¼ teaspoon ground cinnamon

¼ teaspoon ground cloves

¼ teaspoon ground cumin

2½ cups chicken stock

1 ounce Mexican chocolate or bittersweet chocolate plus 1 teaspoon sugar

Salt

ENCHILADAS

Oil for softening tortillas

8 corn tortillas

2 cups cooked shredded chicken

½ onion, sliced thinly

2 cups mole sauce

½ cup queso fresco, crumbled

1 Make the mole sauce: Toast the dried chiles in a large skillet over medium heat until fragrant, then transfer to a heatproof bowl and let them soak in hot water for about 15 minutes before you drain them.

2 In the same skillet, heat the oil over medium heat, cook the onion, garlic, almonds, sesame seeds, and torn tortilla and bread until golden, then add the tomato and raisins and cook until softened. Transfer the mixture to a blender along with the softened chiles, cinnamon, cloves, cumin, and 2 cups of the chicken stock, and blend until smooth. Pour this mixture into a medium saucepan, stir in the chocolate and sugar, and let simmer gently for 25 minutes; if it's too thick, add the remaining stock as needed. Season to taste with salt.

Recipe continues

3 For the enchiladas: Preheat the oven to 350°F. Lightly fry the tortillas in oil to soften, then transfer to paper towels to rest.

4 In a medium bowl, mix the shredded chicken and onion with a few spoonfuls of the mole sauce to infuse the flavor, then roll the filling into the tortillas and lay them, seam side down, in a baking dish. Pour the rest of the mole sauce over the enchiladas and bake for 15 to 20 minutes. Finish with crumbled queso fresco.

JAMAICAN SALTFISH

SERVES 4

Saltfish carries the history of Jamaica in its flavor. Once a preserved staple born out of necessity, it's been transformed by local spices, herbs, and peppers into a dish full of life and identity. To sit down with saltfish is to taste the ingenuity, the heritage, and how a community took something simple and made it rich, bold, and worth gathering around.

8 ounces salt cod, soaked overnight

2 tablespoons olive oil

1 onion, sliced

1 bell pepper, sliced

2 scallions, chopped

2 garlic cloves, minced

1 tomato, chopped

Leaves from 1 sprig thyme

Freshly ground black pepper

1 In a medium pot, boil the soaked salt cod for 10 minutes. Drain and flake into bite-size pieces.

2 Heat the oil in a large skillet over medium heat, sauté the onion, garlic, bell pepper, and scallions until softened and fragrant. Add the tomato and thyme and cook until the tomato breaks down.

3 Add the cod and black pepper. Stir gently and let cook for 5 to 10 minutes, so the flavors meld and the cod absorbs the seasoning.

TOSTONES (FRIED PLANTAINS)

SERVES 2 TO 4

I absolutely love fried plantains! It's the perfect complement to so many meat dishes, especially pork, and I'll never turn it down! Fry up plenty, make yourself a hearty plate, sit back, and enjoy!

2 green plantains

Oil for frying

Salt

1 Peel and slice plantains into 1-inch chunks.

2 In a deep pot, fry the plantain chunks in 1 inch of oil until light golden. Remove, flatten with the bottom of a plate, then refry until crispy.

3 Sprinkle with salt and serve hot.

CUBAN PORK

SERVES 6

This dish is unbelievable—well-seasoned and tender! The marinade makes enough for the pork and the yuca, but adding a side of Congri (page 40) puts it on my list of happy place meals. Can you eat it without the sides? Yes. Do I highly recommend you eating it the way I do? **Yes, yes, and more yes!**

FOR THE MOJO MARINADE

1½ cups sour orange juice (I like Badia or Goya; see Tip)

12 garlic cloves, minced

1 tablespoon + 1 teaspoon fresh oregano (or 1½ teaspoons dried)

2 teaspoons ground cumin

1 tablespoon salt

1 teaspoon freshly ground black pepper

¾ cup olive oil

1 large onion, thinly sliced

FOR THE PORK

3 to 4 pounds pork shoulder or pork butt, trimmed slightly but still with some fat

1 cup Mojo Marinade

1 tablespoon salt

1 teaspoon freshly ground black pepper

FOR THE YUCA

2 pounds yuca (fresh or frozen), peeled and cut into 3- to 4-inch pieces

½ cup Mojo Marinade

1 Make the marinade: In a large bowl or blender, combine the sour orange juice, garlic, oregano, cumin, salt, pepper, and olive oil. Whisk or blend until smooth, then stir in the sliced onions.

2 Place the pork in a large dish or resealable bag and pour 1 cup of the marinade over it, turning to coat thoroughly. Cover and refrigerate for at least 6 hours, preferably overnight, allowing the flavors to deeply penetrate the meat.

3 When ready to cook, preheat the oven to 300°F. Remove the pork from the marinade, reserving the liquid and onions. Pat the pork dry and season all over with a bit more salt and pepper. Place it in a roasting pan or Dutch oven, pour the marinade and onions around it, and cover tightly with a lid or foil. Roast slowly for 3½ to 4½ hours, basting occasionally, until the pork is fall-apart tender and easily shreds with a fork. For a crispy top, uncover during the last 20 to 30 minutes and let the surface brown.

4 Once done, let the pork rest for 10 to 15 minutes, then shred the meat and drizzle with some of the pan juices.

5 While the pork cooks, heat the Mojo Marinade over low heat and prepare the yuca: Bring a large pot of salted water to a boil and add the yuca pieces. Cook uncovered for 20 to 25 minutes, or until the yuca is tender when pierced with a fork. Drain carefully, then remove any tough, fibrous core from the center of each piece. Arrange the cooked yuca on a serving dish. Pour the heated mojo sauce over the warm yuca, making sure each piece gets coated. Let it sit for a few minutes to absorb the flavor, then sprinkle with fresh cilantro or parsley before serving.

TIP: If you can't find sour orange juice, you can make your own by adding 6 tablespoons each lime juice and lemon juice to ¾ cup of orange juice.

FRENCH LADY CAKE

SERVES 6 TO 8

Malinda Russell's French Lady Cake shows just how refined and ambitious her cooking could be. I noticed that her book was heavy on cakes and that made me think about how families often wanted her to help them celebrate. I couldn't help but imagine that she knew how to make people feel special and seen and cared for. I love that idea, being part of people's celebratory moments as a tool to help them love themselves and to be proud of such times. That's a beautiful sentiment and worthy of a cake's being made.

1 cup (2 sticks) butter, at room temperature, plus more for cake pan

2 cups sugar

6 large eggs

3 cups all-purpose flour

2 teaspoons baking powder

1 cup milk

1 teaspoon pure vanilla extract or rose water (more traditional flavoring)

1 Preheat the oven to 350°F.

2 In a large bowl, cream the butter and sugar together until light and fluffy. Add the eggs, one at a time, beating well after each addition. In a medium bowl, sift the flour and baking powder together. Add the flour mixture to the butter mixture in three parts, alternating with the milk, beginning and ending with the flour. Stir in the vanilla.

3 Pour the batter into a buttered 9-by-13-inch cake pan and bake for 35 to 40 minutes, or until a toothpick inserted into the center comes out clean. Remove from the oven and let cool before slicing.

GINGER COOKIES

SERVES 6

Malinda Russell's ginger cookies are a glimpse into the flavors she cherished and the way she took simple ingredients and turned them into something memorable. They're humble and they hold sweetness in every bite. It's a perfect little cookie with an old-school flair. She was on to something.

1 cup (2 sticks) butter, softened, plus more for pan

1 cup sugar

1 cup molasses

2 teaspoons ground ginger

1 teaspoon ground cinnamon

1 teaspoon baking soda dissolved in 2 tablespoons warm water

About 4 cups all-purpose flour (enough to make a soft dough)

1 Preheat the oven to 350°F.

2 In a large bowl, cream together the butter, sugar, and molasses until smooth. Stir in the ginger, cinnamon, and dissolved baking soda. Add the flour, a little at a time, until a soft dough forms. Roll into small balls and place on a buttered baking sheet, flattening slightly.

3 Bake for 10 to 12 minutes, until the edges are set but the centers are still tender. Remove from the oven and let cool before serving.

KNAFEH HONEY PASTRY

SERVES 6

In high school, we had a potluck in Spanish class and we all were picking things to bring. If you made a dish from the Spanish culture, you'd get extra credit, and obviously, because I was always struggling, I chose the extra credit. My classmate Mohammed, on the other hand, did not choose the credit; he chose to bring something that he loves that his mom made at home from the Arabic culture! That was the first time I saw him serious and excited (he was more of a class clown). He got really serious when explaining the dish and how they use honey a lot in their culture and how he loved when his mom made it. We saw a different side of him that day and it was because of the food; the food ushered in that bonding moment with Mohammed and me. You could tell he felt accepted and seen in that moment; he even watched me eat it to see my response, and when I said how good it was, his face lit up. I'll never forget that moment—worlds merged instead of colliding that day.

8 ounces kataifi dough (shredded phyllo), thawed

½ cup (1 stick) butter, melted, plus more for pan

1½ cups shredded mozzarella or string cheese

½ cup ricotta or akawi (if less salty)

½ cup honey or sugar syrup

1   Preheat the oven to 375°F.

2   Toss the kataifi dough with the melted butter. Press half into a buttered 9-inch pie pan.

3   Combine the mozzarella and ricotta in a medium bowl. Spread the cheese mixture evenly over the dough, then top with the remaining dough.

4   Bake for 30 to 35 minutes, until golden. Drizzle with honey or sugar syrup while warm.

ARABIC BREAD PUDDING

SERVES 4 TO 6

This is the most delicate bread pudding I've ever tasted. I almost want to call it polite. Its sweet and light texture makes you want to sit back and soak up each bite with your eyes closed and enjoy the flavor!

5 to 6 croissants, puff pastry, or slices of white bread, torn

2 tablespoons melted butter

4 cups whole milk

½ cup sugar

1½ teaspoons pure vanilla extract

½ teaspoon ground cinnamon

Pinch of ground cardamom (optional)

1 to 2 teaspoons rose water (optional)

1 cup heavy cream

2 tablespoons powdered sugar

½ cup chopped nuts (pistachios, almonds, walnuts), plus more for garnish

¼ cup raisins or chopped dates

1   Toast the torn bread in melted butter in a skillet on the stovetop or on a baking sheet in the oven until golden. Remove from the heat and let it cool completely.

2   In a saucepan over medium heat, heat the milk, sugar, 1 teaspoon of the vanilla, and the cinnamon and cardamom (if using), until just simmering. Remove from the heat and stir in the rose water (if using). Let the mixture cool to room temperature.

3   In a medium bowl, whip the heavy cream with the powdered sugar and remaining ½ teaspoon of vanilla until soft peaks form. Chill until ready to use. Layer the toasted bread, with the nuts and raisins, in a deep dish. Pour the cooled milk mixture over everything. Cover and refrigerate for at least 4 hours or overnight. Before serving, spread the sweetened whipped cream on top and garnish with extra nuts. Serve cold.

CHAPTER THREE

AMERICAN CLASSICS

When it comes to everything in life, find out where you fit best.

Many times, people leave the kitchen discouraged because they feel they don't fit or that they can't be taught. If I had a dollar for each person I taught how to cook, who started out saying, "I can't cook; I can burn water," I'd have very fat pockets. I always bring up life on earth and how it requires fight or flight to survive this land, so it was implanted in us during creation. If we got that because we needed it to live, what about food? Think about it: If that's so, it's only logical to assume that, because we need food to live, there's a natural cook within us upon creation! My thought is that every person just needs to find the spot they fit in best. That's where the biggest problems are created. (You gotta know that I'm gonna connect this to our entire lives in a moment.) I believe some are naturally a baker; for instance, I remember back in culinary school at the top of the semester, I could pick out the bakers—they always had a specific demeanor. Even the students who'd focus on classics, breads, meats, and grilling, and oh boy, the high-fire cooks had a vibe you couldn't deny. The mixologist types were like the bakers; they were always leaning more toward simple science, and they had a feel for what would work in an interesting way.

I found out after a few years of cooking as an adult that I was a savory cook. I did bake, but more so if someone asked me to or needed it. I love the high-heat, short order–style cooking. That's why you'll notice my recipes are often not too lengthy in steps. I get disinterested with too many processes. Finding out where I fit in the kitchen freed up space to deal with anything else that was intimidating me and getting in the way of executing flavor. That was my thing; maybe for others, the thing that could be stopping you from thinking you have a place in the kitchen is a family member who tried to teach you something but who didn't have the capacity to teach, and it left you feeling as if you couldn't be taught. And what about the relative or loved one who leaves out steps in the recipe because they don't want yours to come out like theirs? It's on the laughable side, but it's a thing! Listen, I tell elders who cook that the mac and cheese recipe they're hoarding ain't gonna make it to the afterlife; share it, please, for the love of the table.

I know for my own life, finding where I fit in any area was trying but necessary. It eases up unnecessary fumbles. It's important to look at things in and out of the kitchen as living, just living, not trying to wrap your identity into a task or skill. It's important, too; it'll keep you being nice to yourself, loving, and accepting. It's just food; the painful learning curve in any area, including the kitchen, is just a moment, but you—you're a lifetime. Be gentle with yourself, put the pot on the stove, and find your place.

The following recipes are straight-up favorites for holidays, family get-togethers, and anytime you want something easy to serve.

BLUEBERRY SMOOTHIE

SERVES 2

This is my go-to smoothie, and it's super flexible! Switch out the fruits for whatever flavor you'd like. Get creative and enjoy making great choices!

1 cup frozen blueberries

½ banana

½ cup plain or vanilla yogurt (or a dairy-free version)

½ cup milk or almond milk

1 teaspoon honey or maple syrup (optional)

A few ice cubes (optional)

1 Add the blueberries, banana, yogurt, and milk to a blender. Blend on high until completely smooth and creamy, stopping to scrape down the sides if needed.

2 Taste and add a touch of honey or maple syrup if you'd like extra sweetness, then blend again briefly. Add ice, if desired, for additional thickness and blend for a few seconds.

3 Pour into a glass and serve immediately.

BLUEBERRY MUFFINS

MAKES 12 MUFFINS

I absolutely ADORE blueberry muffins, even store-bought ones. I really think it's a muffin that can do no wrong, in my eyes. One year in high school, it was a thing to bring a cake of some sort to school to share with others, to celebrate. Well, I decided for my birthday to bring in blueberry muffins my mama made for me, and I actually sold them all, all 24 of them. They were that good! That was another wink at my future in the food business for sure! I still have a soft spot for blueberry muffins that I don't think will ever leave me, because they're too good in flavor, and because of the memories attached to them as well.

1½ cups all-purpose flour

¾ cup sugar

2 teaspoons baking powder

½ teaspoon baking soda

½ teaspoon salt

⅓ cup oil or melted butter

1 large egg

½ cup buttermilk

1 teaspoon pure vanilla extract

1 cup blueberries

1 Preheat the oven to 375°F. Line a standard 12-muffin tin with paper liners.

2 Mix together the flour, sugar, baking powder, baking soda, and salt in a medium bowl. In a large bowl, whisk together the oil, egg, buttermilk, and vanilla.

3 Pour the flour mixture into the buttermilk mixture. Stir just until mixed. Fold in the blueberries.

4 Spoon into the muffin pan and bake for 20 to 22 minutes, until golden and a toothpick inserted into the center of a muffin comes out clean.

BUTTERMILK COFFEE CAKE

SERVES 6

When I was a little girl, I used to gather 27 pennies because a Little Debbie coffee cake, which was 25 cents plus tax, was one of my favorite Little Debbie cakes! It would legitimately bring me joy to take that wrapper off to enjoy that little cake. Well, today as an adult, I still love coffee cake as one of my top 5 baked goods. Now, this recipe is the real deal; it takes me where I wanna go whenever I eat it, back down memory lane.

2 cups all-purpose flour

1 cup sugar

1 tablespoon baking powder

½ teaspoon baking soda

½ teaspoon salt

1 cup buttermilk

½ cup melted butter, plus more for baking dish

2 large eggs

1 teaspoon pure vanilla extract

TOPPING

½ cup brown sugar

1 tablespoon ground cinnamon

2 tablespoons butter

Powdered sugar for serving

1 Preheat the oven to 350°F.

2 In a medium bowl, mix together the flour, sugar, baking powder, baking soda, and salt. In a large bowl, whisk together the buttermilk, melted butter, eggs, and vanilla. Pour the flour mixture into the buttermilk mixture and stir until just combined.

3 Pour the batter into a buttered 9-inch square baking dish.

4 In a small bowl, stir together the brown sugar, cinnamon, and butter, then sprinkle over the batter in the baking dish.

5 Bake for 30 to 35 minutes, until a toothpick inserted into the center comes out clean.

6 Sprinkle with powdered sugar before serving.

Homemade Coffee Essentials

HOMEMADE COFFEE CREAMER

SERVES 10 (2 TABLESPOONS PER CUP)

In my world of allergic reactions to random things, this is heaven sent!

**One 14-ounce can sweet-
ened condensed milk**

**1½ cups whole milk
(whole or plant-based)**

**1 to 2 teaspoons pure
vanilla extract, or
another extract (hazel-
nut, caramel, etc.)**

1 In a small bowl, whisk together the sweetened condensed milk, whole milk, and vanilla until smooth.

2 Store in a jar or bottle in the fridge for up to 7 days.
Shake before use.

HOMEMADE CONDENSED MILK

SERVES 4

Holiday time will have you spent in circles in the South if you shop late for your menu! Condensed milk is one of the things people can buy up first, because every house has a pie being made! Well, this is the solution, and I'm more than sure that back in Malinda's time, this is how they made it from scratch, because having milk in a CAN on a shelf wasn't a thing at the time. Why not go back to basics from time to time? This will also serve you well if you have food allergies like I do! Since I'm allergic to dairy, I switch out butter in favor of vegan butter and substitute plant milk for dairy milk in recipes all the time. You would never know! Let this recipe save the day.

1 cup whole milk (use oat or soy milk for vegan)

⅓ cup sugar

1 tablespoon butter (use vegan butter or coconut oil for vegan)

½ teaspoon pure vanilla extract (optional)

1 In a small saucepan, combine the milk and sugar. Simmer gently over low heat, stirring often, until the mixture reduces by about half and thickens slightly, 30 to 40 minutes.

2 Stir in the butter and vanilla (if using). Remove from the heat and let cool, stirring occasionally while cooling, to keep it smooth. It will thicken more as it cools. Store in the fridge for up to 1 week.

TIP: If making vegan condensed milk, soy or oat milk gives the best creamy texture. Almond or coconut milk work, too, but will be thinner.

BUTTERMILK LEMON PEPPER WINGS

SERVES 4 TO 6

When the milk spills and life gives you lemons, make buttermilk lemon pepper wings.

I've had so much milk spill and tripped over so many lemons in the past few years, you'd think I was a lemon farmer whose main mode of transportation was a cow. Listen to me close: It's all in how we process the moments. I don't belittle them or tuck them away. I let the hard times be what they are, and I'm incredibly honest with myself and the parts that my choices played in the pains.

Once I sift through all the parts, I wash my hands and start over in that very second; I don't wait. It's important to show your mind that you trust it by acting quickly. Often, we go through things and we say harsh things to ourselves and disguise it as self-correction, when really it's us punishing ourselves for choices by saying, "That was stupid," or "I should have known better." That verbiage communicates distrust for future interactions with our mind—after that, when our mind decides to warn us, it's a little harder to listen.

Now, if we would accept the spilled milk, and process how it spilled, we'd see how to not let it happen again. What if we dug our heels in deep when the sour lemons arrive, squinted our eyes, and saw how that sour moment ushered in something good, even if it's just a lesson learned? What would we have? I can tell you one thing for sure: We'd have a better quality of time. I think because things perish, we just think of time as being alone by itself. There are levels and tones that we should consider, when choosing and processing moments. We should get in the habit of asking ourselves, "What will I do with this 'spilled milk' or these 'lemons?'" I can tell you what I've learned to do: make something damn good out of it.

2 pounds chicken wings

3 cups buttermilk

2 teaspoons salt

2 teaspoons freshly ground black pepper

2 teaspoons garlic powder

LEMON PEPPER BUTTER

3 tablespoons butter, melted

1 tablespoon lemon pepper seasoning

1 teaspoon lemon zest

Pinch of cayenne

1   In a large bowl, marinate the wings in buttermilk, salt, black pepper, and garlic powder for at least 2 hours (refrigerated overnight is best).

2   Drain and roast or air fry at 425°F until browned and crisp.

3   Make the lemon pepper butter: In a bowl large enough to hold the wings, mix together the melted butter, lemon pepper, lemon zest, and cayenne. Toss the hot wings with the lemon pepper butter.

CAJUN STICKY WINGS

SERVES 4 TO 6

These wings will never fail you if you have to choose a sauce! It's rare for me to turn down wings, and I never turn down these. Keep paper towels near and be sure you make enough wings, especially if they are the main! Sometimes, my kids just enjoy eating wings alone! No sides. Just wings and a drink! They're that good!

2 pounds chicken wings

1 tablespoon oil

3 tablespoons Cajun seasoning

½ teaspoon smoked paprika

STICKY GLAZE

2 tablespoons honey

1 tablespoon hot sauce (Crystal or Louisiana-style)

1 teaspoon Worcestershire sauce

2 garlic cloves, minced

1 teaspoon Dijon or Creole mustard

1 In a large bowl, toss the wings in the oil, Cajun seasoning, and paprika. Roast or air fry until crisp.

2 Prepare the glaze: In a medium saucepan, combine the honey, hot sauce, Worcestershire sauce, garlic, and mustard and simmer until thickened.

3 Toss the wings in the glaze and return to the oven for 5 to 7 minutes, to caramelize.

GARLIC PARMESAN WINGS

SERVES 4 TO 6

It feels like every time I prepare these, they barely make it out of the pan and they rarely cool down before they're gone! I love heavy garlic on anything, though. Sometimes, when I'm giving a recipe on the fly to someone, I'll say, "Add, like, a fistful of garlic," and I mean it! These wings are high on my comfort food list; I'm sure they will be on yours, too!

2 pounds chicken wings

1 tablespoon oil

1 teaspoon garlic powder

Salt and freshly ground black pepper

GARLIC PARM SAUCE

4 garlic cloves, minced

3 tablespoons butter

¼ cup grated Parmesan cheese, plus more for serving

1 tablespoon chopped fresh parsley

Zest of 1 lemon (optional)

1 In a large bowl, toss the wings in the oil, garlic powder, salt, and pepper. Bake at 425°F or air fry until golden and crisp.

2 Prepare the Garlic Parm Sauce: In a large skillet over medium heat, sauté the garlic in the butter until fragrant. Remove from the heat and stir in Parmesan, parsley, and lemon zest (if using).

3 Toss the wings in the warm sauce. Serve with extra grated cheese on top.

HONEY BBQ WINGS

SERVES 4 TO 6

There's always someone who's at the house who asks for BBQ sauce when it comes to chicken, and it makes sense! I think, if you're not normally a sauce person, you will still enjoy honey BBQ wings! You can't resist the tangy and sweet combo, and you can top it with freshly ground pepper at the end for a kick, if you like!

2 pounds chicken wings

Salt and freshly ground black pepper

Onion powder

Garlic powder

BBQ GLAZE

½ cup thick BBQ sauce

2 tablespoons honey

1 teaspoon smoked paprika

1 teaspoon cider vinegar

½ teaspoon chili powder

1   Season the wings with the salt, pepper, onion powder, and garlic powder, then roast at 425°F or air fry until crisp and golden.

2   In a medium saucepan over medium heat, heat the BBQ sauce, honey, paprika, cider vinegar, and chili powder together until smooth and sticky.

3   Toss the wings in the sauce, then broil or bake again for 5 to 7 minutes, until lacquered and rich.

BETTER THAN YA DADDY'S RIBS

SERVES 6

These ribs are the absolute best!! I started making sauceless ribs because it took me a while to become a fan of sauce and condiments in my twenties, and I had a few run-ins with bland ribs that made me want to try out an idea: What if we seasoned them so well we don't need sauce? Seasoned them the way we do chicken? You'd have ribs that would knock someone's daddy off the grill!

1 rack pork baby back ribs
    (2–3 pounds)

2 tablespoons olive oil

2 tablespoons smoked paprika

2 teaspoons garlic powder

2 teaspoons onion powder

2 teaspoons kosher salt

1 teaspoon freshly ground black
    pepper

½ teaspoon cayenne (optional)

4 tablespoons (½ stick)
    unsalted butter

12 garlic cloves, minced finely

Juice of ½ lemon

1 tablespoon chopped fresh
    parsley (optional)

1 Preheat the oven to 300°F.

2 Remove and discard the silver skin from the back of the ribs. Pat dry, then rub with the olive oil. In a small bowl, mix together the paprika, garlic powder, onion powder, salt, pepper, and cayenne, if using, then coat the ribs evenly with the seasoning mixture.

3 Wrap the ribs tightly in foil (meat side up) and place on a baking sheet. Roast for 2½ to 3 hours, until fork-tender.

4 While the ribs roast, melt the butter in a small skillet over medium-low heat. Add the garlic and cook gently until fragrant but not browned, 1 to 2 minutes. Stir in the lemon juice, remove from the heat, and set aside.

5 Remove the ribs from the oven and carefully unwrap. Brush the garlic butter generously over the ribs. Broil, uncovered, for 3 to 5 minutes, to lightly caramelize the top. Watch closely so the garlic doesn't burn.

6 Sprinkle with the parsley, if using, before serving.

"Where there's smoke, there's fire" is a quote to be taken seriously.

In life, we often take smoke as the warning or suggestion, when really the smoke is a preface for the flames right around the corner. We think because we see the smoke, we are safe until the fire appears, but the fire is a quick death and the smoke is a slow and painful one. The smoke can show up years later to cause you pain. So, in the words of my sister Elise, "I'm not interested in being a fireman; I've learned, where there's smoke, there IS fire"—run.

GRILLED CHICKEN SLIDERS

SERVES 8

Sliders are at the top of the list for great handheld bites for a gathering focused on comfort and mingling about the room! It's really a low-effort add-on for a party menu or easy weeknight dinner. I'd partner it with good sea salt kettle chips salt or homemade fries! You've got a good night and a room of happy, full bellies.

1½ pounds boneless, skinless chicken thighs or breasts (cut to slider size)

2 tablespoons olive oil

1 tablespoon freshly squeezed lemon juice

2 garlic cloves, minced

1 teaspoon smoked paprika

1 teaspoon onion powder

½ teaspoon chili powder or cayenne

Salt and freshly ground black pepper

8 slider buns, toasted

TOPPINGS (MIX & MATCH)

Sliced pickles

Coleslaw or shredded lettuce

Tomato slices

Cheese (Cheddar, pepper Jack, or provolone)

Garlic mayonnaise, BBQ sauce, or chipotle aioli

1 In a bowl, toss the chicken with the olive oil, lemon juice, garlic, paprika, onion powder, chili powder, salt, and black pepper. Marinate for 30 minutes, if time allows.

2 Preheat a grill or grill pan to medium-high. Grill the chicken for 4 to 5 minutes per side, until charred and cooked through. Let rest for a few minutes, then slice or leave whole if small.

3 Place the chicken on the toasted buns, add your desired toppings and sauce, then serve warm.

SOUTHERN CORNBREAD DRESSING

SERVES 6

Dressing is more than just a holiday dish in the South—it's tradition, comfort, and family all baked into one pan. In New Orleans and across the South, no Thanksgiving or Sunday spread feels complete without it. Unlike stuffing, which is cooked inside the bird, dressing stands proudly on its own, made with crumbled cornbread, vegetables, and stock and baked until golden. It is the dish that sits at the center of the table and often holds the most memories—the one your mama seasoned with her hand, your auntie perfected with a little sage, and your grandma baked in a pan you swore had magic in it.

1 large pan cornbread (about 8 cups, crumbled)

4 cups day-old bread (white sandwich bread or French bread), cubed

½ cup (1 stick), plus more for baking dish

1 large onion, chopped finely

3 celery ribs, chopped finely

1 bell pepper, chopped finely

1 tablespoon poultry seasoning (or a mixture of dried sage, thyme, and rosemary)

1 teaspoon salt, or to taste

½ teaspoon freshly ground black pepper

3 to 4 cups chicken stock (or turkey stock, if you have it)

2 large eggs, lightly beaten

1 Bake a large pan of cornbread the day before, so it has time to dry out a bit.

2 Preheat the oven to 375°F.

3 Crumble the cornbread into a large bowl, then add the cubed bread. In a skillet over medium-high heat, melt the butter and sauté the onion, celery, and bell pepper until softened and fragrant. Pour the vegetables and melted butter over the bread mixture. Stir in the poultry seasoning, salt, and pepper. Slowly add the stock, starting with 3 cups, mixing until the dressing is moist but not soupy. Taste and adjust the seasoning. Stir in the beaten eggs, then spread the mixture in a buttered baking dish. Bake for 35 to 45 minutes, until the top is golden and set in the middle.

It's YOUR table.

CRISPY POTATO SALAD

SERVES 4 TO 6

When I was a child, potato salad was one of the few things I had to eat fresh while it was still warm. As soon as my mama finished adding the seasonings, I wanted a bowl because I wasn't a fan of cold potato salad. Now, as an adult, I can eat cold potato salad, but I just prefer it to have some crunch or for it to be on the chunky side, so crispy potato salad was the perfect combo! One day, I cooked roasted potatoes and ate a few crispy ones and thought about a coating being on it but with a mayo richness, and that's when I had the idea to try it as a chunky potato salad! I added carrots because I love a raw cold crunch, like crisp lettuce or cold veggies. The best part is that this salad holds some of the firmness when it cools, and it's still delicious! Let me tell you, the shredded carrots are optional, but will blow your mind altogether!

2 pounds baby potatoes, halved

2 tablespoons olive oil

Salt and freshly ground black pepper

Cajun seasoning (optional)

½ cup sour cream or Greek yogurt

1 tablespoon prepared mustard

1 garlic clove, grated

2 tablespoons chopped chives or green onions

3 to 4 cups shredded carrots (optional)

1 tablespoon olive oil (optional)

Freshly squeezed lime juice (optional)

1   Preheat the oven to 425°F.

2   In a medium bowl, toss the potatoes in the oil, salt, and pepper (or Cajun seasoning). Arrange in a single layer on a baking sheet and roast in the oven for 30 to 40 minutes, until crispy.

3   In a separate medium bowl, mix together the sour cream, mustard, garlic, and chives.

4   Toss the roasted potatoes in the dressing while warm. Serve warm or room temperature.

5   If using the carrots, toss the shreds in the olive oil and season to taste with lime juice, salt, and pepper. Lay the carrots on the plate and add the potatoes on top! Thank me later.

Sides & Salads

Sides and salads don't just fill the plate, they complete the meal. In Southern homes, and especially in New Orleans, the side dishes often steal the show. A scoop of potato salad next to fried chicken, a pan of cornbread dressing at the holidays, or a crisp salad with flavors that brighten up a heavy spread—these are the quiet heroes of the table.

What I love about sides and salads is the way they bring balance. Sometimes, they're creamy, cool, and comforting. Other times, they're sharp, tangy, and refreshing. They carry stories, too: recipes passed down, borrowed, or reinvented. These dishes often travel well from one culture to another, changing just enough to fit a new home while still carrying the soul of where they began.

For me, cooking these sides feels like building harmony. They're the parts of a meal that make everything else shine. And whether you're bringing a bowl of potato salad to a barbecue, tossing a green salad for a quick weeknight dinner, or stirring together something new with flavors you've never tried before, the message is the same: Food is meant to be shared.

CARAMEL APPLE PIE

SERVES 4 TO 6

This was the pie I chose to make in culinary school when our baking class had a pie day. My professor, chef Ruth Varisco, gave us a few pie options to pick from, so I chose apple pie because it was my favorite! I could keep it simple, because at each class she gave out "Best of Day" and I aimed to get it most of the time, so I would go above assignment every time. This time, I decided to make a caramel-glazed crust, and it did just what it was supposed to do! Chef Ruth loved it and it was one of the best pies that day! Mission accomplished.

PIECRUST (FOR A 9-INCH DOUBLE CRUST)

2½ cups all-purpose flour, plus more for dusting

1 teaspoon salt

1 cup (2 sticks) cold unsalted butter, cut into cubes

6 to 8 tablespoons ice water

FILLING

6 cups cored, sliced apples (a mixture of Granny Smith and Honeycrisp)

½ cup sugar

¼ cup brown sugar

1 teaspoon ground cinnamon

¼ teaspoon freshly grated nutmeg

2 tablespoons all-purpose flour, plus more for dusting

1 tablespoon freshly squeezed lemon juice

⅓ cup caramel sauce, plus more for drizzling

2 tablespoons butter, cut into pieces

EGG WASH

1 large egg

1 tablespoon water or milk

1 Make the crust: Whisk together the flour and salt in a large bowl. Add the cold butter cubes and cut them into the flour, using a pastry cutter or your fingertips, until the mixture resembles coarse crumbs with pea-size pieces of butter. Sprinkle in the ice water, 1 tablespoon at a time, mixing gently until the dough just comes together. Divide in half, shape into two disks, wrap, and refrigerate for at least 30 minutes.

2 Preheat the oven to 375°F. On a lightly floured surface, roll out one disk of dough into a 12-inch-diameter circle and fit it into a 9-inch pie plate. Then, make the filling: In a large bowl, toss the sliced apples with the sugars, cinnamon, nutmeg, flour, lemon juice, and caramel sauce until well coated. Fill the piecrust with the apple mixture and dot the top with butter pieces. Roll out the second disk of dough and cover the filling with a top crust or lattice, trimming and sealing the edges.

3 For the egg wash, beat the egg with the water or milk in a small bowl, then brush a thin, even layer over the crust. Bake for 50 to 60 minutes, until the crust is golden brown and the filling is bubbly. Remove from the oven and let cool slightly before drizzling with extra caramel and serving.

PECAN PIE

SERVES 6 TO 8

My sister Elise can make one of the best pecans pies I've ever tasted. Honestly speaking, her pie is the reason I started eating pecan pie! She doesn't know that, either; well, now she'll know. I really believe pecan pie should always be served with ice cream. Picture it: warm, sweet pie with creamy ice-cold ice cream to chase every bite. Heaven, right? However you decide to eat it will leave you more than satisfied, I'm sure!

1 cup light corn syrup or pure
    maple syrup

1 cup brown sugar

3 large eggs

2 tablespoons melted butter

1 teaspoon pure vanilla extract

¼ teaspoon salt

1 unbaked 9-inch piecrust

1½ cups pecan halves

1   Preheat the oven to 350°F.

2   In a medium bowl, whisk together the syrup, sugar, eggs, butter, vanilla, and salt until smooth.

3   Pour into the piecrust. Top evenly with the pecan halves.

4   Bake for 50 to 55 minutes, until set and golden. Remove from the oven and let cool completely before slicing.

GRAHAM CAKE

SERVES 6 TO 8

Malinda's Graham Cake was around long before "whole-grain" or "healthy baking" were buzzwords; she was already using graham flour in her cakes. That says a lot about her creativity and her awareness of how food could nourish and not just delight. To me, baking this cake feels like a quiet nod to the fact that our ancestors were innovating with ingredients in ways that still inspire us today. It's simple, hearty, and full of history in every bite.

1 cup (2 sticks), at room temperature, plus more for pan

2 cups sugar

4 large eggs

3 cups graham flour (or whole wheat flour, if graham is unavailable)

2 teaspoons baking powder

1 cup milk

1 teaspoon pure vanilla extract

1 Preheat the oven to 350°F.

2 In a large bowl, cream the butter and sugar until light and fluffy, then beat in the eggs, one at a time.

3 In a separate large bowl, sift together the graham flour and baking powder.

4 Add the flour mixture to the butter mixture in three parts, alternating with the milk, beginning and ending with the flour. Stir in the vanilla until just combined.

5 Pour the batter into a buttered 9-by-13-inch baking dish and bake for 30 to 35 minutes, or until a toothpick inserted in the center comes out clean. Remove from the oven and allow to cool before serving.

CHAPTER FOUR

SNACKS AND SALADS FOR CASUAL GATHERINGS

Let me start by saying it's so much easier than it seems when you try it my way. Whether this intrigues you or makes you roll your eyes, either way, hear me out. My motto is "Work smarter, not harder," when it comes to entertaining, and I always aim to focus on leaving enough space to still have a good attitude for company. Here's how I do it:

First, break up with the idea that order is the evil warden of time and freedom. Many stray away from being organized with many things because, truthfully, it feels a little too close to the order that was pushed on us as children. I think the best way to reconcile with the idea of order and organization is to come to the realization that those two things aren't burdensome and rob you of freedom; they actually remove burden and give you more freedom. I'm always told how effortless I make things seem; it's because I plan everything that allows me to do so. Look, I was a person who hated rules; I felt it was stifling and I was honest enough to call myself out on it. I just got tired of feeling that I could never get close enough to the things I wanted. I would watch people who would get things I wanted and I saw something consistent: plans. They all purposed and planned for those things, and I knew it wasn't a fluke; it was a formula. I tried it once and I was like awww, yeah baby!!! I want ALL the results I can have out of every area of my life!

It's showtime! Pick the most time-consuming or largest item to buy, which is usually the protein or dessert. I never ever feel bad about buying items, not at all. Pick a place most people love, and you're set. I always suggest doing the sides yourself, to save money and then use the saved money on dessert, unless you have a few trusted friends who can be assigned to pick up a thing or two. Choose two or three drinks: water, lemonade, sweetened tea or water, and house punch. You can also keep it incredibly simple and have flavored water—the fewer options, the better!

I'm a big pencil-and-paper to-do list person; I make a checklist for every event gathering or television appearance! That's how I rarely I forget things, because I check them off as I go with a list of supplies, things that need to be cooked or picked up, and the decor. I never decorate the day of, always a day or two before, depending on what my days are like. If things can be cooked a day ahead, I do that or cook early in the morning, so it won't spoil sitting on the counter all day if I don't have the fridge space. The day of is for last touches and small errands, if I have them.

When people arrive, I feel good and look chill, because all of that workload wasn't done in 20 hours.

So, make a list, check it twice, and have a great time. There's a powerful bonding that happens with gathering; if you don't feed the bond, it will break. You can't expect closeness to grow when you're always energetically or physically apart. We saw the wonders a video call service like Zoom could do during the quarantine. Nothing can stop us from gathering and loving on each other; it adds to your bucket of wealth.

WEDGE SALAD PLATTERS

SERVES 4

Wedge platters have to be one of the easiest platter ideas on the planet! Can you imagine, a platter full of wedges, toppings already staged, three types of dressings, garlic bread, and wine? Honey, that's dinner for a group served! It can be as simple as you want!

1 head iceberg lettuce

½ cup dressing of your choice

½ cup cherry tomatoes, halved

¼ cup red onion, sliced thinly

¼ cup cooked crumbled bacon

Freshly ground black cracked pepper

1 Remove any wilted outer leaves from the lettuce. Cut the lettuce head in half through the core, then cut each half in half again, to make four wedges. Trim the core, if you want, but leave a bit to keep the wedge intact.

2 Place the lettuce wedges on a platter. Drizzle each with dressing, then sprinkle with tomatoes, red onion, and crumbled bacon. Finish with pepper and serve chilled.

SALAD DRESSINGS

SERVES 6 TO 8

RANCH

There's no flex like making ranch dressing from scratch and keeping it in a pretty bottle in your fridge. Let's be honest, it feels a little "boss." It also saves you a drive to the store, saves the moments when you don't want to leave the house . . . and having big flavor on demand come straight from the palms of your hands is a godsend. It's definitely a keeper!

½ cup mayonnaise

½ cup sour cream

½ cup buttermilk (or milk with a splash of lemon juice)

1 teaspoon dried dill

½ teaspoon garlic powder

½ teaspoon onion powder

Salt and freshly ground black pepper

Whisk together the mayonnaise, sour cream, buttermilk, dill, garlic powder, onion powder, and salt and pepper to taste in a bowl until smooth. Chill for 15 minutes before serving. Keep refrigerated.

THOUSAND ISLAND DRESSING

This is my younger daughter's favorite dressing! Believe it or not, she uses this for French fries and fried chicken! When I was younger, Thousand Island and Italian were the only dressings I touched; my oldest two children love ranch! I bet it's the creamy and tangy combo that grabs the youth. It's delicious and they are on to something!

½ cup mayonnaise

2 tablespoons ketchup

1 tablespoon sweet pickle relish

1 teaspoon distilled white vinegar

½ teaspoon sugar

Pinch each of salt and freshly ground black pepper

In a bowl, stir together the mayonnaise, ketchup, relish, white vinegar, sugar, salt, and pepper until smooth. Chill before serving. Store in the fridge.

ITALIAN

A tangy classic is always good for the dinner table, because you never know, and you count on a few people who like Italian! You can use this as a chicken breast marinade, just the same as you'd do with any other marinade, as well. I aim for one dressing that's along the lines of Italian by taste and that has a creamy consistency, and suits every guest. It takes just moments to throw together, so it's a win all across the board!

½ cup olive oil

¼ cup red wine vinegar

1 tablespoon freshly squeezed lemon juice

1 teaspoon dried oregano

½ teaspoon garlic powder

½ teaspoon onion powder

½ teaspoon dried basil

½ teaspoon salt

¼ teaspoon freshly ground black pepper

½ teaspoon sugar or honey (optional)

Whisk in a small bowl or shake together in a jar the olive oil, red wine vinegar, lemon juice, oregano, garlic powder, onion powder, basil, salt, pepper, and sugar (if using) until well combined. Refrigerate and shake before each use.

HONEY MUSTARD

Honey mustard is one of the only dressings I will pick as a dipping sauce because of the sweet-with-a-touch-of-sour kick. It's simple; you probably have all the ingredients in your kitchen already! Try it!

¼ cup Dijon mustard

¼ cup honey

2 tablespoons mayonnaise

1 tablespoon cider vinegar

Pinch of salt

In a bowl, whisk together the mustard, honey, mayonnaise, cider vinegar, and salt until smooth. Chill before serving. Store in the fridge.

CLASSIC CAESAR

Caesar will always be a favorite of mine because of its bold flavor! You also feel like a full-on professional, adding anchovies to your salad dressing. It's one of the most important dressings because a Caesar salad is served used as a whole meal. Learn this one and keep it close.

2 anchovy fillets, minced

1 small garlic clove, minced

1 large egg yolk

1 tablespoon freshly squeezed lemon juice

1 teaspoon Dijon mustard

⅓ cup olive oil

2 tablespoons grated Parmesan cheese

Salt and freshly ground black pepper

In a small bowl, mash the anchovies and garlic into a paste. Whisk in the egg yolk, lemon juice, and mustard. Slowly whisk in the olive oil until creamy. Stir in the Parmesan. Season to taste with salt and pepper. Keep chilled.

KITCHEN COUNTER WISDOM
Sometimes, you only have enough arm strength to carry your own bags. It's okay to let every man fend for himself. It's okay to care about YOU.

VEGGIE PLATTER

You don't have to stick with these three, but I picked them because these are all filling veggies that present beautifully! I went with three flavor profiles, and you can just mimic that: sweet, smoky, and garlicky. Have a protein and a bread to go along with it, to close the circle.

HONEY-ROASTED CARROTS

SERVES 4

What I love about this dish is how something made completely from scratch can be as simple as it gets. Just a few ingredients: fresh carrots, honey, a little salt and pepper, and the oven does most of the work. It's proof that cooking doesn't always have to be complicated to feel special. These honey-roasted carrots bring color and balance to the table, whether served at a holiday feast or slipped alongside a weeknight meal. Sometimes, the simplest steps make the most memorable dishes.

1 pound (try to find the colorful ones) carrots, whole or peeled and halved

2 tablespoons olive oil

2 tablespoons honey, plus more to finish

½ teaspoon ground cumin or dried thyme, plus more to finish (optional)

Salt and freshly ground black pepper

1 Preheat the oven to 450°F.

2 On a baking sheet, toss the carrots with the oil, honey, cumin or thyme (if using), and salt and pepper to taste.

3 Roast for 25 to 30 minutes, until caramelized and tender, turning once at around the 12-minute point.

4 Drizzle with extra honey or sprinkle with herbs, to finish.

SMOKY GARLICKY BROCCOLINI

SERVES 2 OR 3

Broccolini may look delicate, but when you roast it with garlic and a touch of smoke, it takes on a boldness that surprises you. This dish is all about letting simple ingredients—garlic, oil, seasoning—speak loudly, and heat. From scratch, it only takes a few steps, but the end result tastes layered and complex, the kind of side that feels at home next to a grilled steak or a pan of roasted fish. To me, this recipe is a reminder that vegetables don't have to play quiet in the background; with the right treatment, they can take center stage.

1 bunch broccolini, trimmed

2 tablespoons olive oil

3 garlic cloves, sliced thinly

½ teaspoon smoked paprika

Salt and freshly ground black
　pepper

1　Preheat the oven to 425°F.

2　On a baking sheet, toss the broccolini with the olive oil, garlic, paprika, and salt and pepper to taste. Roast for 15 to 20 minutes, until tender and slightly charred.

WHOLE ROASTED CAULIFLOWER

SERVES 4

The first time I made a whole roasted cauliflower was for a friend's wedding party, and to my surprise, the kids loved it more than anything else on the table. That tells you a lot about the flavor. Most people don't expect to see a whole head of cauliflower served this way, and that's part of the magic. It takes a simple vegetable and turns it into something beautiful, almost centerpiece worthy. It tastes as good as it looks!

1 whole cauliflower, leaves trimmed (I left mine on for styling purposes)

Salted water

¼ cup panko bread crumbs

1 tablespoon olive oil

½ teaspoon garlic powder

¼ teaspoon smoked paprika

Salt and freshly ground black pepper

2 tablespoons butter, melted

1 Preheat the oven to 425°F.

2 Meanwhile, boil the whole cauliflower in salted water for 10 to 12 minutes, until fork-tender but not falling apart. Drain and pat dry. Place the cauliflower on a baking sheet.

3 In a small bowl, mix the panko with the olive oil, garlic powder, paprika, and salt and pepper to taste. Brush the cauliflower with the melted butter, then press the panko mixture over the top and sides.

4 Roast for 20 to 25 minutes, until golden and crisp.

DIPS

Good dips are communal: They keep people dipping, engaged, and talking. When that happens, memories and good moments are birthed, and it's a beautiful thing. For centuries, gathering over food has been one of the most genius ways to help groups bond and connect. Think about it: Food is one of the top human needs, and up next for your mental, spiritual, and emotional needs is human connection. At the base level, human connection fosters a sense of belonging, reduces stress, and improves self-worth. You see, we all need one another. We aren't designed to be alone socially and emotionally. Physically, we can, sure, but what will that quality of life be? What will those hard times look like with no one to lean on? A group of people to share happiness or your gains in life with— that's what I want to encourage you to build. Coming together and enjoying one of our greatest and most precious needs outside of air and water: food. But let's make it really good food.

PESTO DIP

SERVES 4

Pesto is one of the simplest and most impressive dips you can come by. All you really need is hot bread ripped into pieces, and it feels like you're at a restaurant. It's one of the most diverse dips; you can use as a dip or throw hot pasta into it and toss it around for dinner. It's a win!

1 cup fresh basil leaves

⅓ cup grated Parmesan cheese

¼ cup toasted pine nuts or walnuts

1 garlic clove

Salt and freshly ground black pepper

⅓ cup olive oil

2 to 3 tablespoons Greek yogurt or sour cream (optional)

1 In a food processor, blend together the basil, Parmesan, nuts, garlic, and salt and pepper to taste.

2 Stream in the olive oil, while blending, until smooth. Stir in the yogurt, if using, for a creamier dip.

3 Serve with veggies, bread, or crackers.

OLIVE OIL DIP

SERVES 4

My sister Emma loves polished simplicity, and nothing says that more than an olive oil dip. Let's start with how gorgeous it is to see the seasonings sitting in the oil! On a plain white plate in the center of a table with bread staged on the side? Maybe have different cheeses and fruit to pick from as well? Oh, what about a good red and white wine on the side? You see it, don't you? Do it!

1 garlic clove, grated finely

1 teaspoon balsamic vinegar or freshly squeezed lemon juice

½ teaspoon dried oregano

Pinch of red pepper flakes

½ cup good-quality olive oil

Salt and freshly ground black pepper

Grated Parmesan cheese for garnish (optional)

1 In a shallow dish, mix together the garlic, vinegar, oregano, and red pepper flakes.

2 Pour in the olive oil, add salt and black pepper to taste, and stir to blend. Top with Parmesan, if desired.

3 Serve with warm bread.

OYSTER DIP

SERVES 2 (6 IF SERVED LIKE HORS D'OEUVRES ON A CRACKER)

Let me tell you this ahead of time: You need discipline when making this, or you need to make double. It's that good! It is a cute, quick appetizer that's perfect for a dinner where you want to leave an impression but you don't want to work that hard. This dip has never failed me; you can actually put a teaspoon of it on a cracker with chopped green onion and call it a day!

4 ounces cream cheese, at room temperature

1 tablespoon sour cream or mayonnaise

½ teaspoon freshly squeezed lemon juice

½ teaspoon Worcestershire sauce

Dash of hot sauce

Freshly ground black pepper

One 16-ounce can smoked oysters, drained and chopped

Chopped green onions or fresh parsley

1 In a medium bowl, blend together the cream cheese, sour cream, lemon juice, Worcestershire, hot sauce, and pepper.

2 Stir in the oysters and chopped green onions. Chill for 30 minutes before serving.

3 Serve with crackers or crostini.

BABA GHANOUSH

SERVES 4 TO 6

This is so fun to say, if we're all honest, and even more of a good time to eat! The flavor and texture gets me every time with this recipe. I'm not gonna lie—using lightly buttered garlic bread with this feels sinful! Trust me: Once you try it like that, you won't have it any other way!

1 large eggplant

2 tablespoons tahini

2 garlic cloves

2 tablespoons lemon juice

Salt

2 tablespoons olive oil

Smoked paprika or ground
    cumin (optional)

1 Roast or char the whole eggplant until the skin blisters and the flesh is soft. Let cool, then scoop out the insides.

2 Transfer to a blender and blend with the tahini, garlic, lemon juice, and salt to taste, drizzling in the olive oil while blending.

3 Top with a swirl of oil and paprika or cumin, if using, before serving.

RICOTTA DIP

SERVES 4

Y'all, this ricotta dip SLAPS! It's my favorite dip from the cookbook shoot, as well. The lemony, mild cheesiness is mind-blowingly good. It's soooo simple but so perfect in so many ways. Please put a limit on yourself quickly, because as soon as it leaves the oven and you pierce that top golden layer of cheese, it's over! It's so hard to stop eating it; you've been warned!

1½ cups whole-milk ricotta

Zest of 1 lemon

1 tablespoon freshly squeezed lemon juice

1 garlic clove, grated or minced finely

2 tablespoons grated Parmesan cheese

1 tablespoon olive oil, plus more for drizzling

1 teaspoon fresh thyme or rosemary (or ½ teaspoon dried)

Salt and freshly ground black pepper

1 Preheat the oven to 375°F. In a bowl, mix together the ricotta, lemon zest, lemon juice, garlic, Parmesan, olive oil, thyme, and salt and pepper to taste, until smooth and well blended.

2 Transfer to a small oven-safe dish. Drizzle a little more olive oil on top. Bake, uncovered, for 20 to 25 minutes, until warm, slightly puffed, and just golden at the edges.

3 Serve warm with toasted baguette slices, pita chips, or fresh vegetables.

ANDOUILLE SPINACH DIP

SERVES 6

Mama approved! Our mama was over the day I made this—she came out of her sleep to get a taste of it. She said, "You put andouille in the dip? Put me some in a bowl." I gave it to her and, after one taste, she says, "Yeah, Toy [family nickname], that's excellent!" Listen when your mom is a veteran cook and she compliments your food in that way. It doesn't matter if the first part of your day was a dumpster fire; it's all made right after that moment. That day was a good day and I was grateful to have her with me.

½ cup chopped cooked andouille sausage

1 tablespoon butter

2 garlic cloves, minced

4 ounces cream cheese

½ cup sour cream

½ cup cooked spinach (squeezed dry)

½ cup shredded cheese (Cheddar or pepper Jack)

Cajun seasoning

More sautéed chopped sausage for garnish (optional)

1 In a large skillet over medium heat, sauté the sausage in the butter until browned. Add the garlic and cook for 1 minute.

2 Stir in the cream cheese and sour cream until smooth. Add the spinach and shredded cheese.

3 Add the Cajun seasoning and heat through. Serve warm, garnished with additional chopped andouille sausage, if desired, and chips or bread.

GUACAMOLE

SERVES 4

Everyone needs a good guacamole on their roster! It can be a dip, go with a salad, on a taco, nachos, or even a sandwich. I think it's safe to say that guacamole has proved already how much you need it to make the world go 'round!

3 ripe avocados

1 small red onion, chopped finely

1 jalapeño pepper, seeded and minced (or leave in seeds for more heat)

1 small garlic clove, grated or minced finely

Juice of 1 large lime, plus more to taste

½ teaspoon ground cumin

½ teaspoon kosher salt or to taste

¼ teaspoon freshly ground black pepper

1 Roma tomato, seeded and diced

¼ cup fresh cilantro, chopped

1 Cut the avocados in half, remove their pits, and scoop the flesh into a bowl. Mash roughly with a fork, leaving some texture.

2 Add the red onion, jalapeño, garlic, lime juice, cumin, salt, and black pepper. Fold gently until combined. Stir in the tomato and cilantro last, to keep them fresh. Taste and adjust the lime juice and salt as needed.

3 Serve immediately or press plastic wrap directly onto the surface, to prevent browning.

TRADITIONAL SALSA

SERVES 4

It's absolutely impressive to see all these ingredients chopped in a bowl, knowing that you made it yourself! This is a simple recipe made for you to add your own flair to it. You can adjust the heat and get creative if you want, and enjoy!

4 ripe Roma tomatoes

1 to 2 jalapeño or serrano peppers (depending on how spicy you want it)

2 garlic cloves, unpeeled

¼ white onion

¼ cup fresh cilantro

Juice of 1 lime

Salt

1 Roast the tomatoes, peppers, garlic, and onion in a dry skillet over medium heat or under a broiler until blistered and charred, turning occasionally, 8 to 10 minutes. Let cool slightly. Peel the garlic.

2 Blend everything together—pulse for a chunky texture or blend until smooth. Stir in the lime juice and salt to taste.

SALSA VERDE

SERVES 4 TO 6

The green gets me every time, I swear! If I make the traditional red, I like the verde to be made simply, because sometimes it's all about the color and feel for me. The idea of having options does it as well. I would suggest if you make both as I do: make one spicy and one mild.

1 pound tomatillos, husked and rinsed

1 to 2 jalapeño or serrano peppers (adjust for heat)

2 garlic cloves, unpeeled

¼ white onion

¼ cup fresh cilantro

Juice of ½ lime (optional)

Salt

½ avocado, mashed (optional)

1 Roast the tomatillos, peppers, garlic, and onion in a large, dry skillet over medium heat or under a broiler until blistered and soft, turning occasionally, 8 to 10 minutes. Let cool slightly and peel the garlic.

2 Blend everything together until smooth or slightly chunky. Add the lime juice and salt to taste. (If you want it creamier, add half an avocado, mashed, after blending.)

PICO DE GALLO

SERVES 4 TO 6

Homemade pico adds a fresh and cool element to your meals. It drives them to a completely authentic place, a place that takes a few minutes of chopping and mixing to get there. It's delicious, quick, and a simple addition that conveys "I care."

3 tomatoes, diced

¼ onion, chopped finely

1 jalapeño pepper, minced

¼ cup fresh cilantro, chopped

Juice of 1 lime

Salt

1 Mix together the tomatoes, onion, jalapeño, cilantro, lime juice, and salt to taste in a bowl. Let sit for 10 to 15 minutes, to develop the flavor.

2 Serve fresh with chips or tacos.

HOMEMADE NACHO CHEESE

SERVES 4 TO 6

Nacho cheese is the easiest solution for dips, right behind salsa and guacamole! Just about everyone loves nacho cheese, and even though it's a dip, it can elevate an appetizer table by adding one word: homemade. Try it, fall in love, and impress your guests!

2 tablespoons butter

2 tablespoons all-purpose flour

1 cup whole milk, warmed

1 cup shredded sharp Cheddar cheese

½ cup shredded American cheese

¼ teaspoon garlic powder

¼ teaspoon onion powder

¼ teaspoon smoked paprika or cayenne

Salt

Chopped jalapeño peppers or hot sauce (optional)

1   In a medium saucepan over medium heat, melt the butter. Whisk in the flour and cook for 1 minute to form a roux. Slowly whisk in the warm milk until smooth and slightly thickened, 2 to 3 minutes.

2   Lower the heat to low. Stir in both cheeses, a handful at a time, until melted and smooth. Add the garlic powder, onion powder, paprika, and a pinch of salt. Use more milk to thin it out for dipping, or less for drizzling. For a kick, stir in chopped jalapeños or a splash of hot sauce, if desired. Reheat gently with a splash of milk to bring it back to life.

VEGAN NACHO CHEESE

SERVES 4 TO 6

I'm allergic to dairy, so it's either I consume what I want and take a Benadryl, or I behave, eat a dairy-free or vegan option, and stay away from pain. I generally advise cooks to switch out dairy for plant butter just as a courtesy from time to time, but in the dip category, there are usually three options: guacamole, salsa, and hummus. Rarely is there a nacho cheese replacement, so I added one! Nacho cheese is something that just about everyone wants a part of and doesn't want to be left out of the fun!

1 cup peeled, diced gold potatoes

½ cup diced carrot

½ to ¾ cup hot water

¼ cup raw cashews (soaked in water for 1 hour or boiled for 10 minutes)

⅓ cup nutritional yeast

1 tablespoon freshly squeezed lemon juice

1 teaspoon cider vinegar

1 teaspoon garlic powder

1 teaspoon onion powder

½ teaspoon smoked paprika

¼ teaspoon ground turmeric (for color)

1 teaspoon salt, or to taste

½ teaspoon chili powder or hot sauce (optional)

1   In a medium saucepan, boil the potatoes and carrots in salted water until soft, then drain.

2   Add ½ cup of the (fresh) hot water, drained cashews, nutritional yeast, lemon juice, cider vinegar, garlic powder, onion powder, paprika, turmeric, salt, and chili powder or hot sauce, if a bit of kick is desired, to a blender. Blend until completely smooth and creamy.

3   Add more hot water, if needed, for a pourable texture. Taste and adjust the seasoning to your liking.

4   Serve warm. Keeps well in the fridge for a few days.

MARINATED OLIVE & CHEESE PLATTER

SERVES 4 TO 6

These platters are good for meet-and-greets, small-plate gatherings, and gatherings that have low food focus but you definitely don't want people to mingle while being hungry. All perfect fits for wines and spritzers as well. They plate beautifully and don't take much effort or time.

OLIVES

2 tablespoons olive oil

1 garlic clove, smashed

Zest of 1 lemon

1 sprig rosemary or thyme

Red pepper flakes (optional)

2 cups mixed olives

CHEESES

¼ cup olive oil

1 tablespoon distilled white vinegar or freshly squeezed lemon juice

1 garlic clove, smashed

1 teaspoon dried oregano

Red pepper flakes or peppercorns

Fresh herbs (optional)

8 ounces cubed feta, mozzarella, or goat cheese

TO PREPARE THE OLIVES

1   In a small saucepan, heat the oil over low heat with the garlic, lemon zest, rosemary, and red pepper flakes (if using) for 2 to 3 minutes.

2   Place the olives in a heatproof bowl. Toss the warm oil over the olives and let marinate for 30 minutes or more.

3   Serve as part of a snack board.

TO PREPARE THE CHEESES

1   Combine the oil, white vinegar, garlic, oregano, red pepper flakes, and fresh herbs (if using) in a jar.

2   Add the cheese and toss gently to coat.

3   Let marinate for at least 1 hour before serving.

TO ARRANGE THE PLATTER

Arrange your platter with different types of crackers, crostini, and breads. Depending on the temperature of the room, I would place the filled platter on a bed of ice; serving at room temperature is fine, but serving cool is my preference.

"Inviting other cultures to the table is a great way to remain open toward other communities."

I believe honoring your own culture first at the table is important to you feeling comfortable in your own culture and skin. Then, bring other cultures to the table, observe the flavors of their land, then look for similarities, and finally remember that we are all the same and that we just grew up in different places. It's that simple. Think about family members who live in different places; they come into town and have a whole different set of rules they live under. Maybe in one cousin's house, they let you eat as much as you want, whenever you want, and the kitchen never closes; and in the other, there's a lot of kids, so they have a strict kitchen bedtime—once the dishes are clean after dinner, no one better dare to put another dish in the sink!

Think of that same idea, but with cultures, and understand that things feel odd until you understand them. So, the goal is understanding other cultures rather than judging them. Why is understanding cultures important to building community? Because you live in a wide world that goes beyond your own living room. It's the difference between hearing the perspective of a person who's seen a lot of life, and that of a person who's fresh out of the gate with very little experience. The advice will be different, and the point of view will have different tones as well. Invite them all to the table.

FALAFEL SANDWICH BAR

SERVES 4

There's a favorite place I go to in New Orleans for a falafel sandwich, and it's such a clean and filling meal. I thought to myself, This would be great at home for a gathering! *Keep the falafel and pitas in a chafing dish or warmer and line up the toppings in clear or white bowls so you can see the colors, and BOOM, you have a falafel sandwich bar! However you want to dress it works—just eat and be merry!*

1 cup dried chickpeas (soaked overnight, not canned)

½ small onion, chopped

3 garlic cloves

1 cup fresh parsley, or ½ cup fresh parsley and ½ cup fresh cilantro

1 teaspoon ground cumin

1 teaspoon ground coriander

½ teaspoon baking powder

1 to 2 tablespoons all-purpose flour

Salt and freshly ground black pepper

Oil for frying

Homemade Pita (page 152) for serving

Toppings (page 150) for serving

1   Drain the soaked chickpeas well. Place in a food processor with the onion, garlic, parsley, cumin, and coriander. Pulse until finely ground but not pastelike.

2   Add the baking powder and flour, and season with salt and black pepper. Stir and refrigerate for 30 minutes, to firm up.

3   Scoop and shape into small balls or patties. Fry in hot oil (350°–375°F) for 3 to 4 minutes per side until golden brown.

4   Drain on paper towels. Serve warm in pitas with toppings and sauces.

Optional Sandwich Bar Additions

All these add-ons for your sandwich bar are optional, but here are some tasty ideas to inspire you:

SAUCY

Hummus

Tahini sauce (tahini, lemon, garlic, water, salt)

Garlic yogurt or *labneh*

Spicy harissa mayonnaise or *schug*

Baba ghanoush (for a smoky twist)

TANGY + PICKLED

Pickled turnips

Pickled red onions

Pickled cucumbers

Sliced olives

Lemon wedges

FRESH + CRISP

Shredded lettuce or baby greens

Sliced cucumbers

Diced or sliced tomatoes

Red onion slices

Chopped fresh parsley or mint

Cabbage slaw (vinegar-based or creamy)

EXTRAS + CRUNCH

Crumbled feta

Roasted pine nuts

Dukkah or za'atar sprinkle

Red pepper flakes or sumac

Pita chips or crushed falafel, for texture

HOMEMADE PITA

SERVES 4 TO 6 (DEPENDING ON THE SIZE)

The best way to track what you're eating is to make it from scratch. It's really worth it; it changes the way you view the meal and how it feels to watch people enjoy it. All it takes is planning and attention to detail to get the results you want from your kitchen, and the same goes for life. It's all in the details.

2¼ teaspoons active dry yeast

1 teaspoon sugar

¾ cup warm water

2 cups all-purpose flour

1 teaspoon salt

1 tablespoon olive oil

1 In a large bowl, combine the yeast with the sugar and warm water. Let foam.

2 Stir in the flour, salt, and oil. Knead until smooth. Cover with a clean cloth and let rise for 1 hour.

3 If you will be baking the dough, preheat the oven to 475°F. Roll the dough into small rounds. Bake, or heat in a dry skillet over medium heat, for 2 to 3 minutes per side, until puffed.

HUMMUS

SERVES 4

Hummus is a meal prep's best friend! Scoop some into a travel container with some chips, and you're set! Let me tell you, if you make a couple of options, line up different styles of chips, and have salad with wine, you have the makings of a brilliant meeting with light refreshments or maybe a catch-up session with friends. Either way, you can have a great and tasty time.

One 14-ounce can chickpeas, drained (liquid reserved)

2 tablespoons tahini

1 garlic clove

2 tablespoons freshly squeezed lemon juice

¼ teaspoon ground cumin

Salt

2 to 3 tablespoons olive oil, plus more for serving

Paprika for garnish

Combine the chickpeas, tahini, garlic, lemon juice, cumin, and salt to taste in a blender and blend. Add the olive oil and a few tablespoons of the reserved chickpea liquid and blend again until smooth and creamy. Drizzle with more oil and sprinkle with paprika to serve.

VARIATIONS

Heavy Garlic Hummus
- Add three to four roasted or raw garlic cloves instead of one.
- Optional: Add a pinch of garlic powder, for deeper intensity, if desired.

Roasted Red Pepper Hummus
- Add ½ cup of roasted red peppers (jarred or homemade) before blending.
- Use smoked paprika instead of regular, for depth.

Spicy Harissa Hummus
- Add 1 to 2 teaspoons of harissa paste, or to taste.
- Balance the heat with a touch more lemon juice.

Herb Green Hummus
- Add ¼ cup of chopped fresh parsley or cilantro and a squeeze of lime juice.
- Great with a bit of green chile, for a kick.

Sun-Dried Tomato Hummus
- Add ¼ cup of oil-packed sun-dried tomatoes.
- Boost the flavor with a dash of balsamic vinegar.

PALESTINIAN ARAYES

SERVES 4

I absolutely adore meat pies, but this is more than that. When I made this, I felt the time and love that goes into it. Even holding it in your hand and getting that first bite is a heartwarming experience. Some meals convince you that food is a spiritual and edible communication. This is one of them.

1 pound ground lamb or beef (or a combination)

1 small onion, grated finely

2 garlic cloves, minced

1 small tomato, grated or chopped finely

¼ cup chopped fresh parsley

1½ teaspoons ground allspice

1 teaspoon ground cumin

½ teaspoon paprika

½ teaspoon ground cinnamon

Salt and freshly ground black pepper

4 medium-thick pita breads

Olive oil or melted ghee, for brushing

1 In a bowl, combine the ground meat with the onion, garlic, tomato, parsley, allspice, cumin, paprika, cinnamon, and salt and pepper. Mix until well blended, but don't overwork the meat. Let sit for 10 to 15 minutes, to let the flavors blend.

2 Cut each pita in half to have two semicircles, or leave whole if using thin pitas, and gently open to create a pocket. Spread a thin, even layer of the meat mixture inside each pita, pressing lightly so it sticks.

3 Brush both sides of the stuffed pita with olive oil or ghee. Grill over medium heat or cook in a large skillet over medium heat or a 400°F oven until the pita is golden and crisp and the meat is fully cooked inside, 3 to 5 minutes per side. Press gently with a spatula, if needed, to crisp evenly.

TEA PARTY CAKES

SERVES 4 TO 6

Tea cakes are the most adult flex you can have in your recipe repertoire, especially if you're from the South. My grandmother and mama know how to make them. It almost felt like that was a must-know kitchen standard, back in the day. I think, now, this recipe is one that could impress a few elders, especially since you're going to use it to do two things: bake from scratch and gather people you care for to share over something delicious!

½ cup unsalted butter, at room temperature, plus more for molds (optional)

⅔ cup sugar

2 large eggs

1 teaspoon pure vanilla extract or vanilla bean paste

1 cup all-purpose flour

1 teaspoon baking powder

¼ teaspoon salt

⅓ cup milk, plus more for optional glaze

Powdered sugar for glaze (optional)

Vanilla or strawberry extract for glaze (optional)

FLAVOR ADD-INS

Vanilla: Use base recipe as is

Strawberry: Add 1 tablespoon of strawberry jam or puree, and 1 teaspoon of strawberry extract + 1 to 2 drops natural pink food coloring (optional)

Chocolate: Replace 2 tablespoons of the flour with 2 tablespoons of unsweetened cocoa powder

1 Preheat the oven to 350°F and butter or line four to six wells in a mini muffin or small cake molds.

2 In a large bowl, cream together the butter and sugar until light and fluffy. Beat in the eggs, one at a time, then mix in the vanilla. In a medium bowl, whisk together the flour, baking powder, and salt. Add the flour mixture to the butter mixture in batches, alternating with the milk, just until smooth.

3 Divide the batter among three bowls. Leave one plain for vanilla, stir the jam and strawberry extract into another for strawberry, and sift the cocoa powder into the third for chocolate.

4 Spoon into the prepared pans, one flavor per pan, and bake for 14 to 17 minutes, until the tops are set and springy. Remove from the oven and let cool before serving.

5 If you're making the optional glaze, mix some powdered sugar with a little milk, plus vanilla or strawberry extract, and drizzle over the top of the cooled tea cakes.

CUP CAKE

SERVES 6 TO 8

Baking from Malinda Russell's recipes feels a little like time traveling—reaching back, pulling a piece of her kitchen into mine. Her "Cup Cake" isn't what we think of as a cupcake now, but that's what makes it interesting. We get to look back and see what "normal" looked like in a different time period. Simple ingredients, simple steps, and a taste that connects the past to the present. Every time I make it, I think about the path she carved, and how her words let us share in her table all these years later. It's more than a cake, it's a doorway into history.

1½ cups (3 sticks) unsalted butter, at room temperature, plus more for pans (optional)

1¾ cups raisins

1¾ cups dried currants

¼ cup chopped figs

2¾ to 3 cups all-purpose flour

½ teaspoon baking soda

1 teaspoon cream of tartar

2 teaspoons ground cinnamon

2 teaspoons ground cloves

½ teaspoon ground nutmeg

1½ cups sugar

2 to 4 large egg yolks (the more you use, the richer the cake)

2 teaspoons lemon extract or pure vanilla extract

½ cup sour cream

2 large egg whites (or up to 4 for a lighter texture)

1 Preheat the oven to 350°F and line or butter four to six wells of a standard muffin tin.

2 In a small bowl, toss together the raisins, currants, and chopped figs with a spoonful of the flour, to prevent them from sinking during baking; set aside. In a medium bowl, sift together the remaining flour, baking soda, cream of tartar, cinnamon, cloves, and nutmeg. In a large bowl, cream together the butter and sugar until light and fluffy, then beat in the egg yolks, one at a time, followed by the extract of your choice. Alternately add the flour mixture and the sour cream to the butter mixture, beginning and ending with the flour.

3 In a separate bowl, whip the egg whites to soft peaks and gently fold them into the batter. Finally, fold in the floured dried fruits until just combined. Spoon the batter into the prepared muffin wells, filling each about three-quarters full.

4 Bake for 20 to 25 minutes, or until the cakes are golden and a toothpick inserted into the center of a cake comes out clean. Remove from the oven and let cool before serving.

5 Traditionally, these were served plain or with a simple icing made from sugar and whipped egg whites.

PART TWO

CURE WHAT AILS YOU

If we can cause harm to ourselves, then we must have the full capability to heal ourselves as well.

While I was growing up, being healed by a homemade remedy or ritual wasn't at all foreign to me. My mom and great-grandmother, they were the healers. A healer is a person who has the natural inclination to know what's what, when it comes to the body and its functions and malfunctions. My son Emmanuel had a good bit of asthmatic issues, and before I would bring him to the hospital, I would consult with my mama first and sometimes, most times, I'd just drop him off with her for a day. She'd say, "Let me work on him," and he would come back under control without over-the-counter medicine. Her hands are magical, I swear.

Fast-forward to the quarantine, I got a case of bronchitis that would not leave me alone. I'm talking rounds of steroids and prescriptions, and it got so bad that I couldn't lie down at all to sleep, and if I tried, I'd have a coughing fit. Well, of course, my mama said, "You know what would work for you? Goose grease." Okay, so goose grease is a real thing we used to take in the 1980s whenever we had a chest cold of some sort, and yes, it is grease from a goose, mixed with lemon and honey. My response was, "Let's make a version of it," and we did! Oh man, it cleared me right up! Taking it twice a day, drinking tons of cold water, and keeping the house cold were the instructions from my mama, and I did not stray; within a week, I was better and sleeping flat.

Now in the present day, watching our parents age and the effects of the medicines the doctors want to prescribe can be troubling enough to make you dive deeper into a self-healing journey. As a culinarian, I fully believe that food is our Creator's natural medicine, along with spending time in the elements. I believe that if we can harm ourselves, then we must have the full capability to heal ourselves as well. It just takes time and commitment and, believe it or not, trust. We have to trust ourselves to know that we are making the right choices to keep our body safe.

This entire book is centered on providing for yourself and building up yourself and the people around you; healing and remedies are just another layer of help I want to give. With Malinda Russell's mission in mind to make sure everyone is prepared for life, I want to do the same, so here's a solid collection of soups, remedies, and tonics to stock your fridge, freezer, or medicine cabinet, so you can jump-start your healing journey!

CHAPTER FIVE

SOUPS FOR HEALING

Sometimes you don't have the words for someone who is healing because you've given them already, and sometimes there are no words for someone's particular healing journey. In these times, you employ food.

Recently my sister wasn't feeling well and I wanted to help her in the best way I could. After listening to her to describe her situation, I realized that she had already figured out her issues and all she needed was someone to listen and provide soothing comfort. I'll be honest, outside of my children or when I have a partner, I'm not the best at providing quality time as a love language, especially when I'm processing all my own life's movements and changes in real time. However, I knew this was how I could help my sister, so I went straight to the store. My sister has asthma, so I researched the herbs and veggies that would cater to her needs and made her healing food from my heart! She was pleased with my thoughtful gift of my time and focus, and I was pleased that I gave from where I could afford to give.

As in the words of Mariah Carey, "I'm tryna do the best I can with what I GOT." Let's not forget how food has a voice. Let's not forget we need food to live and we need food to heal as well. Notice how it takes days or maybe months for pills or vitamin supplements to kick in, but with food you can notice immediate relief. Nothing against medicine at all, just a different point of view.

Let's heal each other starting at the table.

THE IMMUNITY SOUP
COLD/FLU RECOVERY

SERVES 6

I love to make this, divide it into 16-ounce containers and pop it in the freezer for sick days, and call it a wrap! It's proof that healing can come from your hands and your kitchen. Once you make it, you can decide whether the next time you want to research your own ingredients and mix it up! Don't be afraid; you can heal yourself!

2 tablespoons olive oil

2 leeks, halved and sliced

3 garlic cloves, smashed

One 1-inch piece fresh ginger, sliced

1 cup mushrooms (shiitake + cremini)

½ teaspoon ground turmeric

Freshly ground black pepper

1 tablespoon tamari or soy sauce

4 cups vegetable or chicken stock

Fresh thyme, parsley stems, and a bay leaf, for serving

Freshly squeezed lemon juice, for serving

1. In a skillet over medium-high heat, heat the oil and sauté the leeks, garlic, and ginger until deeply golden and soft.

2. Add the mushrooms and cook until browned and their moisture evaporates. Stir in the turmeric, pepper, and tamari.

3. Add the stock. Simmer, uncovered, for 25 to 30 minutes. Strain, if preferred. Finish with the fresh herbs and a squeeze of lemon.

CARROT & TURMERIC SOUP
INFLAMMATION REDUCTION AND PAIN RELIEF

SERVES 6

If you're dealing with aches and pains, I think this is perfect soup for you! I also think it's a great idea to pick soups and remedies to gift to elders near you, to make them feel loved. Feeling loved is part of the healing process as well!

1½ tablespoons olive oil or coconut oil

1 small onion, chopped

6 garlic cloves, minced

2 tablespoons grated fresh ginger

1½ teaspoons ground turmeric, or 1 tablespoon grated fresh turmeric

1½ pounds carrots, peeled and sliced

4 cups vegetable stock

1 cup full-fat coconut milk

Juice of ½ lemon

Salt and freshly ground black pepper

1 Heat the oil in a large pot over medium heat. Sauté the onion until soft, about 5 minutes. Add the garlic and ginger and cook for 2 to 3 minutes, until deeply fragrant. Stir in the turmeric and toast briefly.

2 Add the carrots and stock. Bring to a boil, then lower the heat and simmer, uncovered, for 20 to 25 minutes, until the carrots are very soft.

3 Blend until smooth, using an immersion blender, or transfer to a regular blender, blend, and return the soup to the pot.

4 Stir in the coconut milk and lemon juice. Season with salt and pepper to taste. Warm through and serve.

DETOX LENTIL SOUP
GUT HEALTH

SERVES 6

Your gut holds all your life's stress. It's food first, and your thoughts and processing styles second. So, make this and then begin to dump your thoughts in a notebook every night and every morning, and midday if you need to. Notice how you feel afterward. You will feel lighter, and the fact that you're directly putting something in your belly will help; it puts the cherry on top. Trust me. It's what you put in your belly and keep in your mind that influences the gut.

1 tablespoon olive oil or coconut oil

1 small onion, chopped

4 garlic cloves, minced

1 tablespoon grated fresh ginger

2 carrots, chopped

2 celery ribs, chopped

1 medium zucchini, chopped

1 cup dried green or brown lentils, rinsed

1 teaspoon ground turmeric

1 teaspoon ground cumin

½ teaspoon smoked paprika

5 cups vegetable stock or water

Juice of ½ lemon

2 cups chopped kale or spinach

Salt and freshly ground black pepper

1 In a large pot, heat the oil over medium heat. Sauté the onion until translucent. Add the garlic, ginger, carrots, celery, and zucchini. Cook for 5 to 6 minutes, stirring often. Stir in the lentils, turmeric, cumin, and paprika. Toast the spices for 1 minute.

2 Pour in the stock or water and bring to a boil. Then, lower the heat and simmer for 25 to 30 minutes, or until the lentils are tender.

3 Stir in the lemon juice and greens. Simmer for 2 to 3 minutes more, until the greens wilt. Season with salt and pepper to taste.

CELERY SOUP
GUT AND MOOD/ENERGY RECOVERY

SERVES 6

Celery does a good job at making you feel clean on the inside. If I had to describe how the soup makes you feel, I'd say "safe" like I'm making the better decision and, man, that counts for something. Have you ever noticed how you feel guilt at times with some food choices? Well, guess what? What you feel while you're digesting your food counts as well. Listen, the body is the most brilliant and remarkable machine in the world. Make this soup, write down your intentions and eat, and take moments to close your eyes to feel yourself making great decisions and being proud of your investing time in caring for yourself. You deserve it.

1 tablespoon butter

1 tablespoon olive oil

1 onion, diced

1 garlic clove

5 celery ribs, chopped

¼ cup white wine (optional)

1 Yukon Gold potato, diced

4 cups vegetable stock

Fresh thyme or dill

A squeeze of fresh lemon juice

Salt and freshly ground black pepper

1 Heat the butter and oil in a large pot over medium-high heat. Add the onion, garlic, and celery and sauté until fragrant and lightly golden. Deglaze with the wine, if using, and let reduce. Add the potato, stock, and thyme. Simmer for 20 minutes.

2 Blend until smooth, using an immersion blender. Finish with the lemon juice and salt and pepper to taste.

THE HEALER
IMMUNE/RESPIRATORY

SERVES 6

This is a soup I'd suggest if you're thinking of gifting a frozen soup to a friend or loved one in need. It has a good flavor as well, and it doesn't take long at all to put together! Keep this near during the cold season and at the top of spring when allergies get high!

1 tablespoon olive oil

1 onion, chopped

3 garlic cloves, smashed

2 carrots, chopped

2 celery ribs, chopped

1 teaspoon miso paste, or
   1 tablespoon Asian fish sauce

4 cups chicken stock

1 cup water

1 bay leaf

Sprigs of thyme and rosemary

2 cups cooked shredded chicken

Juice of ½ lemon

Salt and freshly ground black
   pepper

1 In a large pot, heat the olive oil over medium heat, add the onion, garlic, carrots, and celery and sauté until soft and aromatic, 5 to 6 minutes. Stir in the miso paste or fish sauce and cook for 1 minute.

2 Add the chicken stock, water, bay leaf, thyme, and rosemary. Bring to a boil, then lower heat and simmer gently for 25 minutes.

3 Add the shredded chicken and simmer for a few minutes more, to warm through. Remove the herb stems and bay leaf. Stir in the lemon juice and season to taste with salt and pepper.

MISO GARLIC SOUP
GUT HEALTH/FLU RELIEF

SERVES 6

Miso is filled with probiotics, antioxidants, and micronutrients. It places itself on the gut-health list, but with an impactful flavor attached to it! Miso can have extra sodium, so my advice would be to up your water intake to balance it all and enjoy the goodness!

1 teaspoon sesame oil

5 garlic cloves, sliced thinly

One 1-inch piece fresh ginger, grated

1 green onion, chopped (whites and greens separated)

4 cups vegetable stock or water

2 tablespoons miso paste

Mushrooms, tofu, microgreens for topping (optional)

Chili oil for serving

1 Heat the sesame oil in a large pot over medium heat, then sauté the garlic and ginger until golden. Add the green onion whites and cook for 1 minute.

2 Add the stock and bring to a simmer. Remove from the heat and whisk in the miso paste.

3 Stir in the toppings (if using) and garnish with the green onion greens. Add a splash of chili oil, for heat.

MINERAL BROTH
LYMPHATIC SUPPORT

SERVES 6

This, combined with exercise—such as a 10-minute walk, three times a week—will keep everything flowing on the inside just as it should! I read not long ago that a walk is like a bubble bath for the brain! Consuming mineral broth on top of that is taking the bull by the horns and steering yourself to a healthy future!

1 onion, halved (skin on, for color)

2 carrots, chopped

2 celery ribs, chopped

1 potato, quartered

1 cup dark leafy greens (kale, collards)

½ cup fresh parsley (with stems)

2 garlic cloves, smashed

1 strip kombu (seaweed)

1 teaspoon cider vinegar

10 cups water

Dried mushrooms or peppercorns (optional)

Salt and freshly ground black pepper

1 Preheat the oven to 400°F. Spread the onion, carrots, and celery on a baking sheet and roast for 20 minutes, to deepen their flavor.

2 Transfer the roasted onion, carrots, and garlic to a stockpot, along with the potato, greens, parsley, garlic, kombu, cider vinegar, and water. Add dried mushrooms or peppercorns, if desired. Simmer, uncovered, for 2 hours.

3 Strain, season lightly with salt and pepper, and sip or use as a soup base. Freeze extra for later use.

CHAPTER SIX

ELIXIRS, SYRUPS & TONICS

Raising a glass to Malinda: Malinda and her relationship to cordials.

In the midst of Malinda's wealth of information, she added a series of drink recipes that weren't regular; they were much more: They were cordials. The word "cordial" comes from the Latin *cor*, meaning "heart." Originally, cordials were medicinal herbal mixtures meant to "invigorate the heart" and restore health. In Europe during the Middle Ages and Renaissance, monks and apothecaries steeped herbs, roots, and spices in alcohol or honey water, serving them in small doses as tonics. By the 17th and 18th centuries, cordials had become fashionable across Europe, flavored with spices and citrus carried by trade. They were still thought of as healthful, but they also became social, the kind of thing you'd sip at the end of a meal, what we'd now call a digestif. When the tradition spread to America, cooks adapted it by incorporating local fruits and herbs. Homemade cordials made from strawberries, raspberries, or currants were a way to preserve the harvest, but they were also a gesture of hospitality, shared at gatherings. That's why it moved me so deeply to see Malinda Russell include cordials in her book. For her to write those recipes in 1866 placed her squarely in that long tradition of using drinks to heal, refresh, and bring people together. Her cordials weren't just about flavor; they were about care, resilience, and offering comfort in a glass. So, with that being said, cheers to Malinda and her heart for the people and passion for healing the body.

Here are a few recipes from Malinda's collection that can come in handy during your time of need. With three flavors to choose from you have:

BLACKBERRY: Blackberries have always been a fruit of survival. Something you could gather along fencerows and hedges, turning a handful of wild berries into a medicine, a sweet treat, or a drink to share.

STRAWBERRY: Their bright color, short season, and sweetness have long made them a symbol of joy and celebration. They mark abundance and the sweetness of life.

QUINCE: Quince is one of those old-world fruits that carries a sense of heritage with it. Tough and tart when raw, it softens into something floral and fragrant once cooked, making it perfect for cordials. Historically given as a symbol of hospitality.

These recipes can be used as they were back then, as tonics and digestifs, or if you want, enjoy them as a cocktail. Here's how to use them:

AS A TRADITIONAL TONIC OR DIGESTIF: Cordials were once sipped straight in very small amounts—1 to 2 tablespoons in a small glass, because the alcohol base preserved the herbs or fruit and concentrated the flavor. They were taken almost like medicine, after meals or at bedtime.

AS PART OF A COCKTAIL: Cordials can be used like a flavored liqueur. Add 1 to 2 ounces to a cocktail shaker with spirits (e.g., rum, gin, or whiskey), citrus juice, and ice, then shake and strain. They bring sweetness, fruit, and depth to balance stronger flavors.

AS A MOCKTAIL: For a nonalcoholic version, stir 2 to 4 tablespoons into 8 ounces of cold still or sparkling water. Adjust to taste.

BLACKBERRY CORDIAL

SERVING SIZE (AS A TONIC): 1 TO 2 TABLESPOONS (½ TO 1 OUNCE); MAKES 32 TO 64 SERVINGS
SERVING SIZE (AS A COCKTAIL BASE): 2 OUNCES; MAKES ABOUT 16 SERVINGS

Blackberries are rich in antioxidants, fiber, and vitamins that support heart health and digestion.

1 quart fresh blackberries

1 pound sugar (about 2 cups)

1 teaspoon ground cloves

1 teaspoon ground nutmeg

1 teaspoon ground cinnamon

1 pint brandy or good whiskey

1 Crush the blackberries in a large bowl until juicy. Stir in the sugar, cloves, nutmeg, and cinnamon, then cover and let sit in a cool place for 24 hours, stirring occasionally as the sugar dissolves. Strain the mixture through a fine sieve or cloth, pressing out as much liquid as possible.

2 Stir in the brandy, then bottle in clean glass jars or bottles. Seal tightly and let the cordial rest for at least 2 weeks before using, so the flavors can deepen.

3 Pour 1 to 2 tablespoons into a small glass as a tonic, or use 2 ounces as the base for a cocktail with spirits and citrus juice.

STRAWBERRY CORDIAL

SERVING SIZE (AS A TONIC): 1 TO 2 TABLESPOONS (½ TO 1 OUNCE); MAKES 32 TO 64 SERVINGS
SERVING SIZE (AS A COCKTAIL BASE): 2 OUNCES; MAKES ABOUT 16 SERVINGS

Strawberries are packed with vitamin C and antioxidants to boost immunity and skin health.

1 quart fresh strawberries, hulled and sliced

1 pound sugar (about 2 cups)

1 teaspoon ground nutmeg

1 teaspoon ground cinnamon

1 teaspoon ground cloves

1 pint brandy or good whiskey

1 Crush the strawberries in a large bowl until juicy. Add the sugar, nutmeg, cinnamon, and cloves, stirring until well mixed. Cover and let sit in a cool place for 24 hours, stirring occasionally as the sugar dissolves. Strain through a fine sieve or cheesecloth, pressing to extract as much liquid as possible.

2 Stir in the brandy, then pour into clean glass bottles or jars. Seal tightly and allow to rest for at least 2 weeks before drinking, so the flavors can blend and mature.

3 Sip 1 to 2 tablespoons as a tonic, or use about 2 ounces as a base in a cocktail with spirits, citrus juice, and ice.

QUINCE CORDIAL

SERVING SIZE (AS A TONIC): 1 TO 2 TABLESPOONS (½ TO 1 OUNCE); MAKES 32 TO 64 SERVINGS
SERVING SIZE (AS A COCKTAIL BASE): 2 OUNCES; ABOUT 16 SERVINGS

Quince is full of vitamin C, fiber, and antioxidants that aid digestion and strengthen immunity.

4 large quinces, peeled, cored, and chopped

1 pound sugar (about 2 cups)

1 teaspoon ground nutmeg

1 teaspoon ground cinnamon

1 teaspoon ground cloves

1 pint brandy or good whiskey

1   Place the chopped quince in a large saucepan, cover with water, and simmer over medium heat until tender, 20 to 25 minutes. Drain well and mash to release the juices. Transfer to a large bowl, stir in the sugar, nutmeg, cinnamon, and cloves and cover. Let sit in a cool place for 24 hours, stirring occasionally as the sugar dissolves. Strain the mixture through a fine sieve or cheesecloth, pressing firmly to extract as much liquid as possible.

2   Stir in the brandy, then bottle in clean glass jars or bottles. Seal tightly and allow to rest for at least 2 weeks before drinking, so the flavors can mellow and develop.

3   Enjoy 1 to 2 tablespoons as a tonic, or use 2 ounces in a cocktail with citrus juice and sparkling water.

CORDIAL COCKTAIL

SERVES 1 (SIMPLY MULTIPLY AS NEEDED)

Cordials were once sipped as medicine, but they quickly became part of celebrations, when they were often mixed with spirits and shared in company. This recipe works with whichever fruit cordial you have on hand.

2 ounces fruit cordial (strawberry, quince, or your choice)

1½ ounces gin, white rum, or whiskey

½ ounce freshly squeezed lemon or lime juice

Ice

Sparkling water to top

Fresh fruit slice or herb sprig for garnish

1   In a shaker, combine the cordial, gin, and citrus juice with ice. Shake until chilled, then strain into a glass with fresh ice. Top with a splash of sparkling water.

2   Garnish with a slice of fruit or an herb sprig to match the cordial flavor.

ELIXIR COUGH SYRUP
BEST FOR BRONCHITIS AND ASTHMA

SERVES 20 (1 TABLESPOON PER SERVING)

This is the cough syrup my mama and I came up with, and it's worth a try! This is our version of the old-school remedy called "goose grease."

Juice of 3 lemons (roughly ¼ cup)

¼ cup extra-virgin olive oil

¾ cup local honey (from the area you live in)

1 Combine the lemon juice, olive oil, and honey in a jar or other container that holds at least ⅔ fluid cup. They will separate but don't worry about that, just stir well before each use, if you have to.

2 Take 1 tablespoon as needed and drink lots of cold water.

GARLIC & GINGER COUGH SYRUP

SERVES 20

Old-school remedies save the day often for me. This syrup contains simple ingredients that you trust, and they're easy to get your hands on. Make it, store it, and share it with others!

½ cup raw honey

¼ cup freshly squeezed lemon juice

2 tablespoons grated fresh ginger

1 garlic clove, minced (optional)

Pinch of cayenne or turmeric

1 Combine the honey, lemon juice, ginger, garlic (if using), and cayenne in a small, nonreactive saucepan over medium heat. Heat gently—don't boil. Let steep for 15 to 30 minutes.

2 Strain and pour into a jar. It will keep, refrigerated, for up to 1 week.

3 Take 1 teaspoon every few hours as needed.

ELDERBERRY SYRUP

SERVING SIZE: 1 TABLESPOON (½ OUNCE) DAILY. MAKES ABOUT 32 SERVINGS PER BATCH

A trusted concoction for colds and flu, elderberry syrup is rich in antioxidants and vitamins. Use it as one of the many ways you can help your body fight off bugs.

1 cup dried elderberries

3 cups water

1 cinnamon stick

3 cloves

One 1-inch piece fresh ginger, finely chopped

1 cup raw honey

1 Combine the elderberries, water, cinnamon stick, cloves, and ginger in a medium saucepan over medium heat and simmer for 30 to 40 minutes, until reduced by half.

2 Strain and allow to cool to just warm. Stir in the honey and bottle.

3 Refrigerate for up to 2 months. Take 1 tablespoon daily.

HOMEMADE COUGH DROPS

MAKES 30 TO 40 DROPS

There's so much you have to watch out for in the things you consume to give you relief during your times of sickness or pain. This is an easy way to keep track of what you put into your body. Nature has much of what we need. Sometimes we just have to slow down to see it, and be patient enough to try it and wait for the results. Making your own cough drops is one of those ways to be attentive and selective when it comes to caring for yourself.

1 cup strong herbal tea (ginger, thyme, lemon, or licorice root)

1 cup sugar or honey

1 tablespoon freshly squeezed lemon juice

½ teaspoon ground ginger or cinnamon

Pinch of cayenne for kick (optional)

Powdered sugar

1 Combine the brewed tea, sugar, lemon juice, ginger, and cayenne (if using) in a nonreactive medium saucepan over medium heat until the mixture reaches the hard crack stage (300°F on a candy thermometer).

2 Quickly drop spoonfuls onto parchment paper. Let cool completely.

3 Dust with powdered sugar, to prevent sticking. Store in a dry jar.

HOMEMADE ANTIMICROBIAL

MAKES 24 SERVINGS (24 TEASPOONS)

Raw honey and garlic combine to help fight infection, boost immunity, and soothe the body the old-fashioned way. You can't go wrong!

4 to 5 garlic cloves, chopped finely

½ cup raw honey

1 In a jar, mix the garlic into the honey and let sit overnight at room temperature.

2 Refrigerate and use 1 teaspoon at a time, for immune support.

VITAMIN C SHOTS

SERVES 4; EACH SERVING 2 OUNCES (¼ CUP)

With a boost of citrus and superfoods, these shots deliver a quick hit of vitamin C to help strengthen immunity and energize the body.

Juice of 2 oranges

Juice of 1 lemon

¼ teaspoon camu camu or acerola powder

Turmeric or ginger juice (optional)

1 Stir or blend together the orange juice, lemon juice, camu camu, and turmeric or ginger juice, if using.

2 Drink fresh or store for up to 2 days.

CHAPTER SEVEN

TINCTURES & OTHER REMEDIES

What are tinctures, why are they so effective, and how do I use them? Tinctures are concentrated liquid extracts made by soaking herbs in alcohol (or sometimes vinegar or glycerin) to draw out their medicinal properties. They're a traditional and powerful way to preserve and use herbs for healing. They're effective for a few good reasons and here's why:

FAST ABSORPTION: They work quickly because they absorb directly into your bloodstream under the tongue.

LONG SHELF LIFE: Tinctures last for years, if stored properly.

POTENT AND CONCENTRATED: You need only a few drops to get the benefits.

EASY TO TAKE: No brewing, cooking, or prep—just drop and go.

CUSTOMIZABLE: You can blend herbs to target specific needs, such as sleep, immunity, or stress.

PORTABLE: Small bottles make them easy to carry and use anywhere.

NATURAL OPTION: They're made from herbs, often with minimal processing.

The following is a guide on how to use them day to day.

How to Use Tinctures

Place drops under the tongue or dilute in water/tea. A common dose is 20 to 40 drops, two or three times daily (check specific herb), best taken between meals for faster absorption.

ELDERBERRY (IMMUNE SUPPORT): 2 or 3 times daily during illness

ECHINACEA (SHORT-TERM IMMUNE BOOST): 3 times daily at onset, up to 10 days

ASHWAGANDHA (STRESS, SLEEP, HORMONE BALANCE): 1 or 2 times daily

LEMON BALM (CALMING, DIGESTION): 2 to 3 times daily, as needed

VALERIAN ROOT (SLEEP AID): 1 time daily, 30 minutes before bedtime

MILK THISTLE (LIVER SUPPORT): 2 times daily

CHAMOMILE (GENTLE CALMING): 2 or 3 times daily, or as needed

PEPPERMINT (DIGESTIVE RELIEF): 1 or 2 times daily, before or after meals

GINGER (NAUSEA, INFLAMMATION): 2 or 3 times daily, as needed

TURMERIC (ANTI-INFLAMMATORY): 2 times daily, with food

Shake the bottle before use. Store in a cool, dark place. Check for interactions and discuss with your doctor if on medication.

TINCTURES (WORMWOOD, OREGANO, MULLEIN)

1 TO 2 DROPPERFULS (30 TO 60 DROPS, OR 1 TO 2 ML)
TOTAL SERVINGS: ROUGHLY 120 TO 240 SERVINGS PER 8-OUNCE BATCH
(1 OUNCE = ABOUT 30 DROPPERFULS)

This works as the base method and yield for any tincture.

1 part dried herb, or 3 parts fresh

4 parts high-proof vodka, or cider vinegar for nonalcoholic

1 Fill a glass jar one-third full with your herbs. Cover completely with vodka or cider vinegar.

2 Shake daily. Let steep for 4 to 6 weeks in a dark place.

3 Strain and store in dropper bottles. Take a few drops as needed.

PAIN-RELIEF TINCTURE

A traditional herbal blend crafted to help ease inflammation and soothe aches, combining roots and bark long valued for their natural healing powers.

1 part turmeric root (anti-inflammatory)

1 part ginger root (circulation + pain relief)

1 part white willow bark (natural aspirin-like effect)

1 part devil's claw root (joint + arthritis support)

80- to 100-proof vodka (or brandy), enough to cover herbs

A few black peppercorns (optional; helps activate turmeric)

1 Combine the dried or chopped turmeric, ginger, white willow bark, and devil's claw in a clean glass jar. Cover completely with vodka, leaving about 1 inch of space at the top. Seal tightly.

2 Store in a cool, dark place for 4 to 6 weeks, shaking the jar every few days.

3 Strain through cheesecloth into a clean dropper bottle. Label with its name and date.

HOW TO USE: Take 1 to 2 dropperfuls (30 to 60 drops) under the tongue or in a little water, 1 to 3 times daily, as needed. Not for use without physician guidance—especially if using white willow bark.

STRESS-RELIEF TINCTURE

A calming blend of herbs in tincture form made to ease tension, quiet the mind, and support balance when life feels heavy.

1 part lemon balm (calming, uplifting)

1 part passionflower (relieves anxious thoughts)

1 part chamomile (soothing to body and mind)

1 part ashwagandha root (adaptogen that helps the body handle stress)

80- to 100-proof vodka (or brandy), enough to cover herbs

1 Place the herbs in a clean jar. Pour in the vodka to cover by at least 1 inch. Seal the lid tightly.

2 Store in a cool, dark spot for 4 to 6 weeks, shaking every few days.

3 Strain and transfer to dropper bottles. Label with its name and date.

HOW TO USE: Take 1 to 2 dropperfuls (30 to 60 drops) under the tongue or in a bit of water, up to 3 times a day, especially during stressful moments or to help unwind in the evening.

MENTAL CLARITY TINCTURE

A bright, focusing blend of herbs to clear mental fog, sharpen concentration, and bring steady energy to the mind.

1 part rosemary (stimulates circulation to the brain)

1 part gotu kola (improves memory and cognitive function)

1 part ginkgo biloba (boosts blood flow and alertness)

1 part peppermint (refreshes and energizes the mind)

80- to 100-proof vodka (or brandy), enough to fully cover herbs

1 Place the herbs in a clean glass jar. Cover with vodka by at least 1 inch.

2 Seal tightly and let sit in a cool, dark place for 4 to 6 weeks, shaking every few days.

3 Strain well and pour into dropper bottles. Label with its name and date.

HOW TO USE: Take 1 dropperful (about 30 drops) in water or under the tongue 1 or 2 times a day, especially in the morning or before tasks that require focus.

KITCHEN COUNTER WISDOM

"If you can't take the heat, get out of the kitchen" is a classic lesson of thinking of consequences before actions, and if those consequences seem unbearable to you, don't do the actions. Choices get us into bad situations and circumstances, but the bright side is that choices also get us out of them—and not only do you get out, but you're wiser than ever.

MUCUS-RESOLVING SHOTS

SERVES 2

A quick, fiery blend of lemon, ginger, and cider vinegar to help clear congestion, wake up the respiratory system, and bring fast relief.

Juice of ½ lemon

1 tablespoon cider vinegar

1 tablespoon ginger juice or grated fresh ginger

Pinch of cayenne

Raw honey (optional)

1 In a glass jar, stir or shake the lemon juice, cider vinegar, ginger juice, cayenne, and honey (if using) together. Take 1 ounce daily, or as needed.

2 Store in a small bottle for up to 3 days.

GINGER CHEST RUB

SERVES 12 (1 TEASPOON)

A warming, aromatic rub made with ginger, eucalyptus, and coconut oil to help open airways and ease chest congestion naturally.

¼ cup coconut oil

Beeswax (optional; to help firm up the rub)

2 teaspoons grated ginger or ginger essential oil

10 drops eucalyptus oil

1 Melt the coconut oil and beeswax (if using) in a small pot over low heat. Stir in the ginger and essential oil.

2 Let cool slightly, then pour into a clean container. Store, sealed, at room temperature and use on chest for congestion relief.

KOMBUCHA

SERVES 8

A probiotic-rich tea that supports gut health and delivers a refreshing tang, homemade kombucha is an ancient tradition that's still used and loved today.

4 black or green teabags

1 cup sugar

8 cups water

1 SCOBY + 1 cup starter tea

1 Brew the tea in hot water and add the sugar. Let cool completely.

2 Transfer to a clean jar with the SCOBY and starter tea.

3 Cover with a clean cloth and let ferment for 7 to 10 days. Taste daily until tangy.

ELECTROLYTE DRINK

SERVES 2

A natural way to rehydrate and replenish citrus for vitamin C, with honey for quick energy, and sea salt to restore what your body sweats out.

2 cups water or coconut water

Juice of 1 lemon or orange

1 tablespoon honey or pure maple syrup

Pinch of sea salt

Pinch of baking soda (optional; alkalizing)

1 In a clean glass jar, stir together the water, citrus juice, honey, sea salt, and baking soda (if using) until dissolved.

2 Chill, then sip slowly for hydration support.

OKRA WATER

SERVES 1 OR 2

A simple tonic rooted in Southern and folk traditions, okra's natural mucilage is believed to soothe digestion, balance blood sugar, and refresh the body.

3 to 4 okra pods, sliced

1 to 2 cups water

Squeeze of fresh lemon juice (optional)

1 In a small bowl, soak the okra slices in the water overnight.

2 Strain and drink in the morning, with a squeeze of lemon juice (if using) for digestive or blood sugar support.

CHAPTER EIGHT

BATH & BODY

I loved how Malinda Russell left no stone unturned when it came to sharing the knowledge and expertise she'd gained over the years. It's wonderful to know how to make things so that you can truly track what's going into your body, but the other benefit of knowing how to make medicine and household supplies is saving on monthly expenses.

If you're in a place where you want to cut the costs that can be cut or you or someone you love has been having allergic reactions, making things yourself is one option to start narrowing down the culprit. Take my mama, for instance; as a kid, I kept breaking out with this light rash, so my mama would fill up the tub with a dry milk bath to soothe my skin. The next step was eliminating things I ate to see what caused it, and keeping everything fragrance free. Well, after trial and error, she figured out that anything that had an abundance of red dye number 40 would cause the rash! Yes, you guessed right, that as a kid in the 1980s and '90s, this cut me out of a lot of things that were fun and trendy, but I will say that it was the end of the rashes.

I told you that story to further show you how you can truly take control and guide yourself to healing when it comes to life and the body. I know firsthand from growing up with allergies and having children with them, that when you're consuming a lot of over-the-counter and mass-produced products and food, it becomes a needle-in-a-haystack situation to find out a root cause to an issue. So, this chapter may help during the narrowing-down-causes process. These methods and techniques aren't new. Many of us can remember elders telling us what would work, or making us do things when we were feeling well that seemed extra or silly but actually made us feel better! Let's get back to that place!

HAIRCARE

Malinda really understood that food was just one of the ways of nourishing yourself. When I think back on her book, it also focuses on self-care, including hair remedies and other solutions. She thought of every need, and the idea of food and haircare being in the same book brings me back to my childhood of getting my hair done by my mama in the kitchen. For many Black children, that was our first salon experience. I remember it clearly: My mama would remove everything from the countertop and off the table, set up the shampoo and conditioner, and put towels on the countertop so I could lay across it, with my head tilted back in the sink. She'd wash my hair, and afterward I'd sit on the floor between her legs so she could detangle and comb my hair, getting me ready for the week. This is a story that travels across the Black community, and Malinda knew our story well. I had to add a set of recipes to close the circle on the homage I paid to her throughout this book. Here, you'll find simple recipes for shampoo, conditioner, growth oil, and deep conditioner, all made from scratch with ingredients you can trust. Just like a good meal, these recipes remind us that tending to ourselves is part of the work, too. Taking the time to nourish your hair and body is another way of saying, "I'm worth the time and care."

SIMPLE HOMEMADE SHAMPOO

MAKES 8 TO 10 WASHES, DEPENDING ON HAIR LENGTH

A gentle, all-natural shampoo that cleanses without harsh chemicals, and it's easy to make, customizable with oils or scents, and kind to your scalp.

½ cup liquid castile soap (unscented or mild scented)

½ cup distilled water, or cooled boiled water

1 teaspoon olive oil, jojoba oil, or almond oil (for moisture)

10 drops essential oil (optional; lavender, peppermint, or tea tree)

1 In a clean bottle, combine the castile soap and distilled water. Add the oil and essential oil (if using), then shake gently to mix.

2 To use, pour a small amount into your hand, massage into your wet hair and scalp, then rinse thoroughly.

3 Shake before each use, as natural ingredients may separate. Store in the shower and use within 2 to 3 weeks.

VARIATIONS
- For oily hair, add 1 tablespoon of cider vinegar to help balance the scalp pH.
- For dry hair, increase the oil slightly, or follow with a light conditioner.

SIMPLE HOMEMADE CONDITIONER

MAKES 4 WASHES

A creamy blend of coconut milk, honey, and natural oils to deeply moisturize and soften hair.

1 cup coconut milk (unsweet-ened, full-fat, if possible)

2 tablespoons honey

1 tablespoon olive oil or jojoba oil

5 to 10 drops essential oils (optional)

1 In a clean bowl, whisk together the coconut milk, honey, and olive oil until smooth. Add the essential oil (if using).

2 After shampooing, apply the mixture generously to damp hair, working it through from scalp to ends. Let it sit for 5 to 10 minutes, then rinse thoroughly with warm water. Store leftover conditioner in the refrigerator for up to 1 week.

TIP: For extra moisture, cover your hair with a shower cap and let the conditioner sit for 20 minutes before rinsing.

HAIR GROWTH OIL

MAKES 10 TO 12 APPLICATIONS

A rich blend of oils designed to help stimulate the scalp, strengthen strands, and encourage healthy hair growth.

½ **cup jojoba oil or olive oil (base oil)**

2 **tablespoons castor oil (helps promote thickness and strength)**

1 **tablespoon coconut oil (for moisture)**

1 **teaspoon vitamin E oil (optional; preserves and nourishes)**

10 **drops rosemary essential oil (stimulates scalp circulation)**

5 **drops peppermint essential oil (cooling, helps promote growth)**

5 **drops lavender essential oil (soothes scalp)**

1 In a small glass bottle or jar, combine all the oils. Shake gently to blend.

2 To use, part your hair and apply a few drops directly to the scalp, then massage with your fingertips for 3 to 5 minutes to stimulate circulation. Leave it in for at least an hour, or overnight for a deep treatment, then wash out with shampoo. Store in a cool, dark place. The oil blend will last for several months.

TIPS: Use 2 to 3 times per week, for best results. Warm the oil slightly before applying for better absorption.

DEEP CONDITIONER

MAKES 1 OR 2 APPLICATIONS

Rich with avocado, honey, and yogurt to moisturize, strengthen, and soften hair.

1 **ripe avocado (moisturizing and strengthening)**

2 **tablespoons honey (locks in moisture)**

2 **tablespoons olive oil or coconut oil (nourishing base)**

2 **tablespoons plain yogurt (adds protein and smoothness)**

5 **drops rosemary or lavender essential oil (optional)**

1 In a bowl, mash the avocado until smooth; add the honey, oil, and yogurt until well blended, then add the essential oil (if using).

2 On freshly washed, damp hair, apply the mixture from roots to ends, making sure every strand is coated. Cover with a shower cap and let it sit for 20 to 30 minutes, so the nutrients can soak in. Rinse thoroughly with warm water, then style as usual. Best used fresh, but leftover conditioner can be stored in the fridge for up to 2 days.

TRADITIONAL EPSOM SALTS BATH SOAK

ENOUGH FOR 1 STANDARD BATH SOAK
MAKES 1 BATH (2 CUPS SALTS + OPTIONAL OILS)

A timeless home remedy for soothing sore muscles, calming the nervous system, and offering a simple way to relax body and mind.

2 cups Epsom salts

5 to 10 drops essential oil
(optional; lavender, eucalyptus, or peppermint)

1 Fill your bathtub with warm water. Add the Epsom salts and stir to dissolve.

2 Add the essential oil (if using). Soak for 20 minutes.

TIPS: Hydrate before and after soaking. Rest afterward, for best results.

DETOX BATH SOAK

MAKES 1 BATH

A purifying soak that helps draw out impurities, ease muscle fatigue, and restore balance to the body.

½ cup bentonite clay

¼ cup powdered ginger

½ cup sea salt

1 Mix together the clay, ginger, and salt in a bowl, then transfer to a dry jar to store.

2 Add ½ to 1 cup to a warm bath. Soak for 20 to 30 minutes.

RELAXING HERBAL BATH

MAKES 1 BATH

A fragrant soak of calming herbs that eases tension, quiets the mind, and turns an ordinary bath into a ritual of rest.

½ cup Epsom salts

¼ cup dried lavender or chamomile

5 to 10 drops essential oil of your choice (optional)

1 Combine the Epsom salts and dried lavender or chamomile in a small bowl. If desired, add 5 to 10 drops of essential oil and stir to blend.

2 Spoon the mixture into a muslin bag, cheesecloth, or clean sock and tie it closed. Place it under warm running water as you fill the tub, or drop it directly into the bath.

3 Soak for 15 to 20 minutes , then discard the herbs and rinse the tub.

DRY MILK BATH

MAKES 1 BATH

The milk powders soften the skin, while a warm soak nourishes and leaves you feeling restored. This is something my mama would do if she was itchy after being around grass too long; it would soothe her skin and calm her down.

1 cup powdered whole milk (goat's milk or coconut milk powder also works)

½ cup finely ground oats (colloidal or blitzed in a blender)

¼ cup baking soda (soothes itch and balances pH)

2 tablespoons cornstarch or arrowroot powder (reduces friction and inflammation)

1 Mix together the powdered milk, oats, baking soda, and cornstarch in a medium bowl and transfer to a dry, airtight jar to store.

2 To use, add ½ to 1 cup of the mixture to warm bath water. Stir to dissolve. Soak for 20 to 30 minutes, then pat your skin dry—no rinsing needed.

WHAT THE DRY MILK BATH HELPS WITH
- Eczema flare-ups
- Dry, flaky, or sun-exposed skin
- Itching from heat rash, bug bites, or minor irritation
- General skin softening and moisture barrier repair

CHAPTER NINE

CLEANING REMEDIES

When you first think of making your own household supplies, you immediately wonder whether it will be a daunting process. IT WON'T BE! Oh man, I swear the majority of the supplies are mix or pour and shake and, BOOM! you've saved $10.99!

This stuff actually works, and I'm not gonna lie—it makes you feel a form of confidence. I had a revelation after that surge of confidence, and it was that making these items myself empowered me deeply, because before this point, I was always buying someone else's solutions to my problem, and this time I was solving them myself. It was ther-apeutic once I told on that train of thought, and I trusted myself with myself a little more. It seems like making your own cleaning supplies isn't just about cleaning the home; it's about cleansing the idea that you can't solve your own problems and meet your own needs. I tell you what: Malinda was on to something pretty big.

HOMEMADE WINDOW CLEANER

I use this mix more often than I use store-bought glass cleaner. Honestly, I just get tired of feeling like chemicals are all around me with all the store-bought cleaning products—not to mention getting tired of feeling like I'm spending my money twice after a long cleaning session. I've caught myself thinking, Oh, I can just make more! with a tone of ease. That's what it feels like to make it all from scratch: Your sense of self-sufficiency is restored with a few simple steps. Let's go all the way!

1 cup distilled white vinegar

1 cup water

1 tablespoon rubbing alcohol

5 drops essential oil (optional; lemon, peppermint, etc.)

1 Combine the vinegar, water, rubbing alcohol, and essential oil (if using) in a spray bottle. Shake gently.

2 Spray on glass or mirrors and wipe with a lint-free cloth or newspaper.

ANTIBACTERIAL BATHROOM CLEANER

When I was younger, I felt as if the bathroom wasn't clean unless a loud smell was floating down the hall. Now, as a seasoned adult I know that that strong scent is traveling not just down the hallway but through my body. This cleaner recipe doesn't have many bells and whistles, but it gets the job done the best, quietest, and safest way.

1 cup water

1 cup distilled white vinegar

2 tablespoons baking soda

10 drops tea tree oil

5 drops lemon or eucalyptus oil (for scent)

1 Combine the water and vinegar in a spray bottle.

2 Add the baking soda slowly (it will fizz), then the tea tree and lemon oil. Shake gently before use.

3 Spray on surfaces. Let sit for 5 to 10 minutes before wiping.

NATURAL LAUNDRY DETERGENT

I have always experienced irritation when washing my clothes in fragrant detergent, and so have my children. Wearing clothes shouldn't cause pain or discomfort, and monitoring your detergent can be a big help for narrowing down skin triggers if you easily get skin rashes. This hypoallergenic detergent would be the perfect gift for a baby shower or a new mother!

1 bar castile or laundry soap, grated

1 cup washing soda

1 cup borax or baking soda

½ cup distilled white vinegar (optional)

1 Mix together the grated soap, washing soda, and borax well. Store in a dry, airtight container.

2 Use 2 to 3 tablespoons per load (HE-safe). If using for extra freshness, add the distilled white vinegar to the rinse cycle.

LIQUID DISH DETERGENT

You realize something very simple when going through these cleaning recipes: You already have everything you need for your home at home to make the most of your time! Doesn't that feel grand? Doesn't that make you feel like a responsible, resourceful adult? It feels good, doesn't it? This dish soap is the simplest fix for a sink full of dirty dishes; all you need to add is a pair of hands.

1 cup liquid castile soap

¼ cup distilled water

1 teaspoon baking soda

1 teaspoon lemon juice or vinegar

10 drops citrus or mint essential oil (optional)

1 Mix together the castile soap, distilled water, baking soda, lemon juice, and essential oil (if using) in a squeeze bottle or jar.

2 Shake before use. Use 1 to 2 teaspoons per sink or sponge.

HOMEMADE STAIN SOLUTION
FOR COLORS

Stains happen and this is the solution. Adding this stain solution to a spray bottle is a brilliant addition to your daily laundry needs.

1 cup distilled white vinegar

1 cup warm water

1 tablespoon baking soda

1 tablespoon castile soap or mild dish soap

1   In a large bowl or spray bottle, first mix together the vinegar and water. Slowly add the baking soda (it will fizz), then stir in the soap.

2   Apply directly to the stain. Let sit for 15 to 20 minutes, then blot or scrub gently, and rinse or wash as usual.

HOMEMADE STAIN SOLUTION
FOR WHITES

Whenever you're dealing with stains on white garments, it is best to move as quickly as possible in order to prevent the stain from setting in.

1 cup 3% hydrogen peroxide

½ cup baking soda

1 tablespoon castile soap or mild dish soap

1   In a bowl, mix the hydrogen peroxide, baking soda, and soap into a paste or a pourable blend. Apply directly to stains and gently rub in.

2   Let sit for 30 minutes to 1 hour (longer for set-in stains). Rinse or launder in hot or warm water.

HOMEMADE FLOOR CLEANER
FOR CERAMIC AND TILE

Floor cleaner is something I go through quickly, so making it for myself was the best option! I like to open the windows to let my floors dry; it feels like a fresh reset.

1 gallon warm water

¼ cup distilled white vinegar

1 tablespoon castile soap or mild dish soap

10 drops essential oil (optional; lemon, tea tree, or lavender)

Mix together the warm water, white vinegar, soap, and essential oil (if using) in a bucket. Mop as usual with a damp (not soaking) mop or microfiber cloth. No rinse needed—just allow to air dry.

HOMEMADE FLOOR CLEANER
FOR WOOD FLOORS

Wood floors are my soft spot. I love to see them carefully tended to because they're so beautiful. Double the oil if you want to add more of a shine to your floors.

1 gallon warm water

¼ cup distilled white vinegar (removes residue)

2 tablespoons olive oil or jojoba oil (adds natural shine)

5 to 10 drops essential oil (optional; lemon, orange, or cedarwood)

Mix together the warm water, white vinegar, olive oil, and essential oil (if using) in a bucket. Lightly dampen a mop or cloth (never soak wood). Clean in the direction of the grain, wringing out any excess moisture back into the bucket, as needed. Let air dry or buff with a dry towel. Please note that anytime you're mopping wood floors, you should never use a soaked mop, because the excess moisture will soak into the wood and cause it to break down.

HOMEMADE POTPOURRI

I don't like it when my house smells like food, especially particularly pungent foods like fried foods, gravy, eggs, or popcorn. I will open the windows a few hours before people arrive and then burn a fragrant candle or put a pot of potpourri on the stove to give a beautiful scent to my house. I like people to taste my food and smell my home. Try this homemade potpourri; you and your guests will love it!

1 cup dried citrus peels (orange, lemon)

½ cup dried rose petals or lavender

¼ cup cinnamon sticks or whole cloves

1 tablespoon dried rosemary or mint

a few drops essential oil (for heightened scent)

Mix together the dried citrus peels, rose petals, cinnamon sticks, rosemary, and essential oil and store in a dry jar or uncovered bowl. To refresh the scent, stir occasionally, or add more oil.

"I wanted to make the backgrounds myself, so it could have a from-scratch feel. I purchased a ton of unique and cool all-white plates to keep a clean but edgy vibe. Each time we shot, it genuinely felt like I was my own competition, because I had to challenge myself to use either the same plate or same background differently. Those moments were more significant than I knew now that I'm writing this: I had to show myself what I could do with my mind, my hands, and how I could trust my choices."

I had this vision of a broken plate with a meal on it as a representation of how sometimes good things can fall apart. I shared my idea with someone and they asked me a question that brought everything levels deeper: "Why don't you glue it back together?" I thought, *What a brilliant response. Why don't we simply glue it back?* True, it won't be the same, but it will be a new and beautifully redefined "something" if you let it. Well, time passed and I was talking about the concept to someone and they said, "Hey, that's actually a Japanese art form called *kintsugi*." Now, y'all, at this point it was destiny; this vision I had was telling me something that I knew I had to share with you. Kintsugi, which means "golden joinery," is rooted in the philosophy of *wabi-sabi*, finding beauty in imperfection, and teaches that something can become more beautiful for having been broken. Instead of hiding the broken pieces, they paint them gold and honor the imperfections. Isn't that what Malinda did? Isn't that what we all have to do throughout our lives and hard times? Find the beauty in the cracks and make art out of broken pieces. We are all connected more than we know. We need each other and each other's stories. I promise if we take the time to dig deeper into the journeys of others, we will see how similar we are and how we aren't as alone as we think.

I've decided to take hold of all the broken pieces in my life, glue them together, paint them gold, and display them with honor. I hope you can join me.

In every situation,
aim to be an ocean
without a ripple.

—Toya Boudy

ACKNOWLEDGMENTS

I want to start by acknowledging myself for getting out of my own way. At this point of my life, I've never been so sure and unsure at the same time. With many tears flowing as I write this, I want to honor my bravery and courage.

Notice I didn't say "fearlessness," because fear is and has been present, but I'm proud to say it hasn't stopped me. I keep going, even if I'm crying or uncertain. I keep going and I love that about myself. I thank God for my design, and I'm sorry I spent so long trying to change things about myself that God put perfectly in place. All things that God made are good and I'm one of those things. To my mama, the more I mother, the more I'm in awe of how you did and do what you do for us. I'm grateful you get to see all the hard work you put into me come to life. You deserve your flowers now; I appreciate you. Daddy, thank you for always embracing starting over for the sake of the family, I see you; I know it's not easy. You taught me how to use music and art as my refuge. That saved me many times and I'm sure it will the rest of my life. Watching you start over multiple times has shown me how to not give up on myself no matter what. Daddy, thank you for always facing the music; I respect that about you. Emma and Elise, you're not just my sisters, you're my friends, and I love that God placed me with y'all. Thank you for always cheering me on; your support gives me more fuel than you know. Krystal, there's one thing about us: We're gonna counsel each other through the trenches of starting over, and I'm grateful for you and our connection; you're one of my favorite childhood memories. To Kelly, thank you for your support, love; and endless encouragement; you cheered me on through one of the roughest times of my life. It means the world to me; I'm grateful for you. Chef Ruth, my forever professor, you've went above and beyond the professor title with me, year after year, since we've met. My mother and I thank you for everything that you are to my career and my development as an artist. Ann Triestman, with Countryman Press, for always guiding and supporting me and my vision. My agent, Ellen Sorado, with Stonesong, for supporting me as well. Sam Hanna, it's been a perfect creative fit since the beginning! Thank you for loaning me your brilliant eye. Chris, every project, every business, every major to minor goal, needs a "Chris" excellence that isn't in you, it's you. We did it again! My final acknowledgment goes to the big to tiny humans who call me "Ma" or "Mommy": Heaven, Emmanuel, and Binah Boudy, thank you for being so understanding through my creative process and long hours; trust me, I know it's tough sharing me at times. I love you deeply for allowing me to be who and what I am. Thank you for accepting and loving me through our new beginning.

INDEX